THE MASTER ARCHITECT SERIES IV

Herbert S Newman and Partners

Selected and Current Works

THE MASTER ARCHITECT SERIES IV

Herbert S Newman and Partners

Selected and Current Works

First published in Australia in 1999 by
The Images Publishing Group Pty Ltd
ACN 059 734 431
6 Bastow Place, Mulgrave, Victoria, 3170
Telephone (61 3) 9561 5544 Facsimile (61 3) 9561 4860

National Library of Australia Cataloguing-in-Publication Data

      Herbert S. Newman and Partners, P.C.
      Herbert S. Newman and Partners : selected and current works.

      Bibliography.
      Includes index.
      ISBN 1 86470 052 1.

      1. Herbert S. Newman and Partners, P.C. 2. Architects – United States.
      3. Architecture, Modern – 20th century – United States.
      4. Architecture, American. I. Newman, Herbert S, 1933–. II. Title.
      (Series: Master architect series IV).

  720.973

Edited by Stephen Dobney and Andy Whyte
Designed by ShoemakerDesign with Peter Newman of HSNP, New Haven, CT.
Production by The Graphic Image Studio Pty Ltd,
Mulgrave, Australia
Film by Scanagraphix Australia Pty Ltd
Printed in Hong Kong

Contents

Introduction

By Herbert S. Newman

When I was young my parents wanted me to become a doctor or a lawyer. Both medicine and law, in their eyes, offered a way to contribute to the life of society, to benefit mankind. But at college I discovered art and architecture, and my future wife, and with her urging I enrolled in architectural school.

The world of architecture I entered in the mid 1950s was the architecture of modern masters. At the Yale School of Architecture, I was taught by Louis Kahn, Paul Rudolph, and Joseph Albers. It was a time of true belief in the transcendent power of Modern architecture and individual genius. Surrounded and taught by great architects and architectural historians, imbued by the poetry and humanism of Kahn, the passion and insight of Vincent Scully, and with exciting new buildings changing the campus, architecture students at Yale believed they could achieve great things.

After graduation from Yale, I worked with I.M. Pei for five years, commuting to New York from New Haven, where my wife and I had begun a family. Pei was another of the great Modernists, and I learned much from him and his thoughtful, gifted partner, Harry Cobb. When I began my own practice in the mid 1960s in New Haven, architecture was beginning to change. Yale, where I had started teaching in design, was a crucible for this change. Eero Saarinen's Yale colleges had just been built. Edward Larrabee Barnes had designed an exquisite, unbuilt, "contextual" Master's House for Yale's Old Campus. Charles Moore had become dean of the architecture school; and Robert Venturi, who had recently written *Complexity and Contradiction in Architecture,* was a visiting lecturer and critic. Modern architecture was being challenged by visions of a broader world of architectural possibilities, by an acceptance of heterogeneity, of history, of context, of continuity. It described a set of ideas that seemed more egalitarian, pluralistic, and human than the architecture of orthodox European Modernism, which was born out of a rejection of aristocratic, oligarchic structures that no longer existed.

I identified with much of the new thinking because it resonated with my parents' deeply implanted directive to me that through my work I should be doing good for others. It seemed possible that architecture could again speak a language that would be shared by all those it served; that architecture could be inclusive, familiar, intelligible. The philosophical cornerstone of my practice became the idea that architecture is not only for the gratification of a self-anointed few, but rather that it might be accessible for anyone who experiences it. While this notion and its expression have evolved and developed over the years, what is now a collaborative partnership remains committed to this principle.

Among the many great teachers I enjoyed as a student and young architect were I.M. Pei and Louis Kahn. Pei was then, as he is now, a committed Modernist, but he has a way of infusing his work with a personal and Chinese cultural sensibility that roots his best work in a place that is somehow outside time. Louis Kahn understood, perhaps more than any others of his generation, the permanence of human values that transcend the changing fashions of the times. He spoke of architecture as responsive to human experience that goes beyond temporal utility and program. He developed ideas of hierarchies of path and space ordered by structure and light. He thought about the forces of nature and humanity and their persistent patterns—patterns that mold the world we inhabit.

I mention my beginnings in architecture not only because they were formative, but because they are indicative of the way I continue to acquire understanding in my life's work. What I believe about architecture is largely an outgrowth of my experiences and my reflection upon those experiences, whatever their origins. It is an attempt to understand the nature of human experience and how it shapes and is informed by the physical environment.

My beginnings in architecture also define the way we, in our architectural practice, search for ways to give form to our work. Working with the material of lived experience is how we, as a partnership, have come to approach each project; and it is how we have come to understand the relationship between architecture and society, and between ourselves as individuals and the communities we serve.

We are driven by the hope that what we design will improve the lives of people, make places better for them. While we don't believe in human perfectibility, we want to bring out the best in ourselves and appeal to the best in the people we serve. We want to promote the idea of a better place, made palpable through space and form.

Practicing as we do, with our office on the campus at Yale University, we work within a great collective work of architecture that reminds us daily of the qualities that architecture should have. The Yale campus is imbedded in the street grid of New Haven. Its thoroughfares are also those of the town. It is a remarkable milieu in which to be and to work, because whatever one might think of these buildings individually, collectively they represent and constitute what is great in human culture, and are a description of what can be done when people strive to do their best. The outcome is a setting in which one's capacity for wonder can be deeply plumbed. Like one of those fabulous but evanescent world expositions that used to enliven us with visions of a future architecture, Yale is a model of what can be, but with an architecture that is as permanent as architecture can be—our kind of architecture—not here today and gone tomorrow. Of course, the Yale campus is exceptional; it is not every town, street or city. It is not typical. In most places its quality cannot be repeated, but it is a standard to which we aspire.

Over time, architectural form changes: evidence of the continual searching of the human mind, seeking what is new and seeking other ways to express how we as humans experience and account for life. In our own practice we are influenced by what is interesting to other architects, but we have confirmed through experience that some ideas about architecture are more than existential commentary—they are unchanging. And we have found that although people's interests change, human nature does not. What people fundamentally seek in architecture is always the same. So as we endeavor to design for all people, we endeavor to imbue our work with the elements of architecture which are always true for all people, as my early mentors demonstrated in their work and thought.

All architectural form has to deal with certain fundamental earthbound forces: gravity, wind, earthquakes and water. Gravity wants to level everything, wind to knock everything over, earthquakes to shake everything to ruins, and water to wash it all away. In the face of these immutable tendencies, history attests to the enduring constancy of human nature. We believe, therefore, in architecture's central function: providing shelter with "firmness, commodity and delight" in answer to the eternal forces of both physical and human nature.

We all are aware, as perhaps never before, that the world is a place in constant flux. People move from place to place. Cultural boundaries overlap. Capital moves freely and swiftly. Political structures, which once seemed permanent, have been undone. Recent technological change has transformed whole nations. In our practice, we have a heightened appreciation of the paradoxes within the structure of change and permanence. It is to this question, in each project, that we, as architects, seek an appropriate response.

We design armatures for the changes that architecture needs to acknowledge. Fixed in place are the public paths, stairs, bathrooms, structure and distribution systems for environmental systems. Between these we allow that virtually all other functions in a building be able to change. We believe in this clear and unchanging use of a building's armature. For things to change in meaningful ways, there must also be things that do not change. For change to occur and be understood, it must be compared to that which does not change. For example, the physical structures of Hagia Sophia and the Pantheon are constants which have accommodated change of use while retaining their wonder.

Because human nature is a constant, we try to understand and love people for what they are and do. Therefore, the places we make for them reflect an affection for ordinary human interchange, social intercourse, and commerce. We seek an architecture that accommodates and enhances the pursuit of happiness, the love of surprise, and the instinct for pageantry. To participate in a public activity in a public place and yet hold onto your private identity and sense of self is an experience to be found in all wonderful public places. We aspire to create that quality in our work.

People need to live and interact with one another to retain their humanity. We need places and paths to see and be seen, to observe each other, to converse, to play, to eat, to work, to share ritual and beliefs, to celebrate life and to mourn death. This is a layer of human activity that is often left out of an architectural program. We believe there is often an inchoate or "hidden" program that deals with the serendipitous, urbane, and humanizing experience of rubbing shoulders, of passing each other, of unspoken and spoken communication. Therefore our ideas begin with and take form from the notion of the path. We attempt to establish clear entry portals and circulation systems that enable these events to occur.

People need to belong to something larger. They want to make connections with others and with places to make order out of chaos, to pursue happiness. They want to feel comfortable, both alone and with others. They want settings in which to play out

their destinies. Architecture always needs to represent something larger than either the individual or the group, yet provide places where individuals can both be themselves and understand the social structures in which they are enmeshed.

We believe in the rooting of architecture to its site in a circumstantial way from which a set of ideas—unpredictable ideas—may emerge that locates the circumstantial in a larger order.

We know, of course, that temporal considerations will always inform a work of architecture. They enable us to identify styles, periods, and the cultural settings in which individual works were conceived. These considerations reflect the uniqueness of each of us as well as the uniqueness of our ideas and tastes.

As architects we have the responsibility to ask ourselves: will the place where we will be building be a better place when our building is done? Will the campus, village, city, or open space, be more wonderful? Or, to put it in Hippocratic terms, will we cause no harm? This is important, because as architects we have to accommodate our creative urges within the boundaries imposed by the building type, the program, the site, and an understanding of our own limitations. It is important for architects to test their talent by taking risks, and it is equally important for clients to give architects the opportunity to take risks. It is also necessary to understand the effect of risk-taking on the physical environment, to understand the difference between architectural decorum and architectural banality; between wit and jest; between hoping to be able to visit a place time and again because of the wonder of what it is that we have built, and never giving it another thought after we have taken our well-posed photograph. As architects, we make shelter. We must care for and nurture those we shelter with the same passion and dedication with which we pursue the ineffable.

Colleges and Universities

Lynn University Library

Design/Completion 1993/1996
Boca Raton, Florida
Lynn University
58,000 square feet/200,000-book capacity
Reinforced concrete, plaster stucco

The role of the library in society is changing, and flexibility of space to accommodate rapid change is a fundamental principle guiding state-of-the-art library design. At the same time, the hierarchical ordering elements of public space, circulation, natural light, structural and mechanical systems, and utilities are unchanged.

Lynn University Library was designed to accommodate a collection with a projected total of 200,000 volumes by the year 2010, while directing human activity in ways that are familiar and congenial to learning.

While the library is classical in form and monumental in scale, its materials and building details follow regional traditions. The columns and walls are unadorned stucco in the manner of inexpensive contemporary Florida construction. In response to the heat and sun, windows are set deeply into the walls and shaded with metal screens, while screened, shaded porches at the front and rear reflect the local climate and patterns of building use.

At the entrance to the library is the major information hub. From this place, users find their way to reference librarians, reading rooms, meeting rooms, and support staff. Marking this major point of confluence is a circular stairway illuminated from above by an oculus. Numerous small reading and study areas, interwoven among the open stacks and positioned near windows, provide readers with natural light and views of the outdoors.

The lobby, checkout spaces, and meeting rooms are separate from study areas to ensure quiet. Fully networked for computer and telecommunications access, computer areas and book collections are located in the interior of the library to minimize harmful glare from the Florida sun, and to ease the load on environmental systems.

1

2

3

1   Library forecourt
2   Detail of interior
3   Screen porch reading room
4   Entry elevation
5   Ground floor plan

4

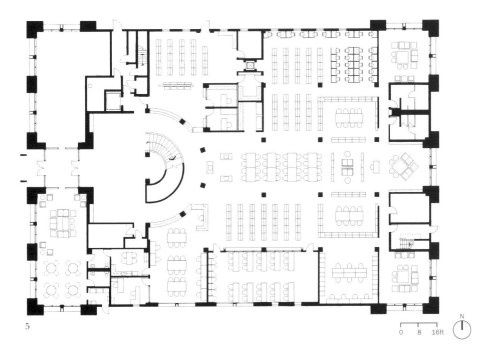

5

0 8 16ft   N

6

6 Second floor terrace
7 Stair to second floor
Following pages:
    Elevation

7

Lynn University
ASSAF Academic Building

Design/Completion 1994/1996
Boca Raton, Florida
Lynn University
17,000 square feet
Concrete, drywall, acoustic tile, aluminum

The campus of Lynn University was designed by Edward Durell Stone in the late 1950s. At the center of the campus, buildings face one another across a linear pedestrian spine. All the original facades have perforated cast concrete block screens, a signature of Stone's work.

The ASSAF Academic Building renovation was part of our master plan to accommodate the physical growth of the university. The project included the renovation of the existing building and the addition of laboratories, forming a new central courtyard.

Our design of the ASSAF Building, which faces the new university library, which we also designed, replaced the block sunscreen with an arched eyebrow of metal at the front door over new horizontal slats. A larger-scale screen celebrates entry and creates hierarchy on the pedestrian spine.

1

Before

1 Building court
2 Entry facade
3 Ground floor plan

2

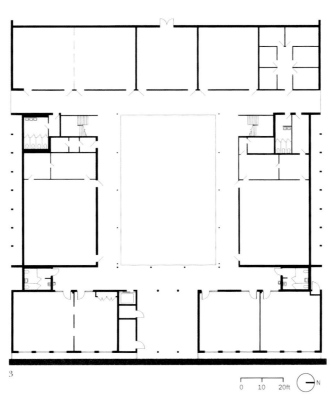

3

Yale University
New Residence Hall

Design/Completion 1997/1998
New Haven, Connecticut
Yale University
124,000 square feet
Brick, precast concrete, lead-coated copper roof

Because this was a design-build project, its budget was about half the cost of a typical residence hall at a private university. We chose simple vernacular forms to express continuity with its residential neighbors and to act as a foil for the monumental Payne Whitney Gym and the University Power Plant.

The new residence hall continues the Yale residential college tradition of low buildings with towers defining courtyards, vistas, and portals. It is brick with a lead-coated copper roof and a mass defined by gables, chimneys, bay windows, and dormers. A central courtyard planted with American elms serves as an outdoor "living room" with informal paths, terraces, and seating.

The hall has 108 two-bedroom apartment suites, each with a kitchenette, living room and bathroom. The suites are arranged along central corridors on four floors in an apartment-style program that allows complete gender separation within a coeducational setting. Activity spaces include lounges, computer rooms, an exercise room, and a common room. This program fosters community and a sense of place for students as well as the university's summer conference residents.

The design reflects our years of research into the behavior patterns of students: their need to make connections with social groups and to establish independence through freedom of choice and privacy, and their desire to see others and be seen by others unselfconsciously in a non-confrontational setting.

The design solves Yale University's dilemma of undertaking extensive renovations to its 12 residential colleges without disrupting the lives of the students who inhabit them. It allows Yale to begin the renovations systematically, one by one, while providing interim housing for the students of each college under renovation. It is the first new residence hall to be built on the campus since 1961.

1

2

3

1   Aerial view of site
2   Elevation from Ashmun Street
3   View from entry across courtyard
4   Site plan

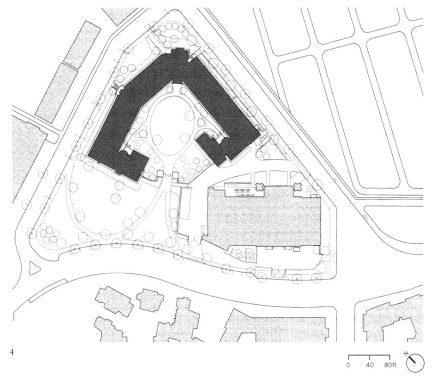

4

0   40   80ft

6

7

Previous pages:
  Entry court portal
6 Common room
7 Ground floor plan
8 Detail

0   20   40ft

8

9

9 Common room stairwell detail
10 Detail of entry gate
11 Third floor common room
12 View from Morse College

10

11

12

New School for Social Research

Design 1985
New York, New York
Parsons School of Design
37,000 square feet (new);
200,000 square feet (renovated)
Steel frame, cast stone, brick, aluminum
window wall, quarry tile

*The New School for Social Research has
a reputation for being in the vanguard of new
ideas. In its renovation we wanted to create a
composition that demonstrates a visual and
contextual duality between the old and the new,
and illustrates how they can nourish each other.*

Located on Fifth Avenue, the new
building replaces a four-story brownstone
with twelve stories of new construction,
linking the three main divisions of the
New School: Parsons School of Design,
the Graduate School of Management and
Urban Professions, and the Adult Division.

The full-height skylight atrium,
constructed within an existing light well,
defines the center of the building group,
forming a new indoor campus. Acting as
the hub, it allows direct connections
between prime areas such as the library,
student cafeteria, and faculty offices.
Circulation spaces ring the atrium,
creating passages which foster chance
or serendipitous meetings by the students
and faculty.

A gallery court below the atrium provides
exhibition and reception capacity, while
allowing access to the street. A "library
court" is connected to it by an open stair,
establishing an area for casual and off-
hours study.

The new façade serves as the main
entrance, with access to all three branches
of the New School. The front building
houses administrative and faculty offices
and teaching spaces—simple lofts
designed as studios for programs such
as communication and graphic arts,
computing, and film and media.

Continuing the celebratory tradition
of using flags as ornament, the large
flagpoles are seen from many blocks away,
establishing the school as a landmark and
announcing its three branches.

1

2

1 Existing building
2 "Flags" by Childe Hassam
3 Model looking South
4 Model looking North

3

26 Herbert S Newman and Partners

Colgate University
Dana Addition, Case Library

Design/Completion 1979/1981
Hamilton, New York
Colgate University
75,000 square feet
(45,000 renovated, 30,000 new)
Steel frame, limestone and brick veneer,
slate roof, painted gypsum board
and oak paneling

When it was built in 1958, the Case Library conformed to the notion of a library as a warehouse for books, and its architectural treatment reflected that idea. With our addition, we gave it a heart, reflecting its importance as the center of learning at the university, and a place for imagination.

Our solution was to hide the existing library behind a 30,000 square foot addition and treat it like a "bustle" behind the new mass. This gave the library new prominence on the campus, forming a stone and brick facade that makes it compatible with the surrounding mid-nineteenth century Georgian and Victorian architecture.

The new two-story central reading room that is now the library's heart offers students a variety of reading spaces, ranging from alcoves to an attic loft, providing for group or individual study. We doubled the library's seating capacity, expanded the stack areas by one-third, and tripled the microfilm area. We renovated the music listening room, added a communications studies room, and expanded staff work rooms. We later installed sprinklers and air conditioning, and replaced the original windows.

Our new design provided better circulation from information to the card catalogue to the reference stacks, updated the library's systems, and confirmed a hierarchy that accords the library an elevated place in the world of learning.

1

2

1   Library facade
2   Side elevation
3   Lawn view
4&5 Sections

3

Before

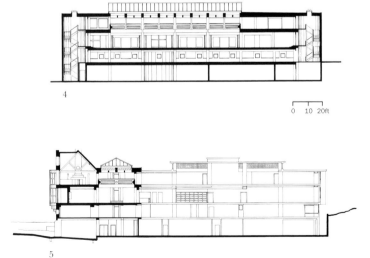

4

0 10 20ft

5

7

8

6&7   Reading room
   8   Second floor study carrel

Colgate University
Curtis Frank Dining Hall

Design/Completion 1981/1983
Hamilton, New York
Colgate University
27,000 square feet/500 seats
Steel frame with brick and stone veneer,
slate roof, skylights, drywall, oak, quarry tile,
slate and carpet flooring, brick interior partition
with wood trim, brick fireplaces

*Ideas first explored in our work at Yale
University's Donaldson Commons dining hall
are further examined here, primarily the
"sidewalk cafe phenomenon" and the need for
students to make connections and establish a
sense of belonging.*

Located at the end of a major pedestrian
axis, Curtis Frank Dining Hall evokes a hill
town, with the roof of the main hall acting
as a "cathedral," and the dining rooms
acting as components of a "village." Most
seating is along the edges of paths defined
by low walls and banquettes, providing
privacy with a view of the surroundings.

Because Hamilton's winters are typically
snowy and gray, the interior spaces
enliven the mood by collecting and
diffusing natural light. The building acts
as a natural light fixture, so artificial light
is rarely needed during daylight hours.

Anticipating heavy use of the dining hall,
we used wood and masonry interior
surfaces capable of developing a patina
over time. The building is set on a scenic
wooded campus among existing native
stone buildings with gabled slate roofs.

1

2

1   North side elevation
2   Detail
3   Entry facade
4   First floor plan
Following pages:
   Entry view

3

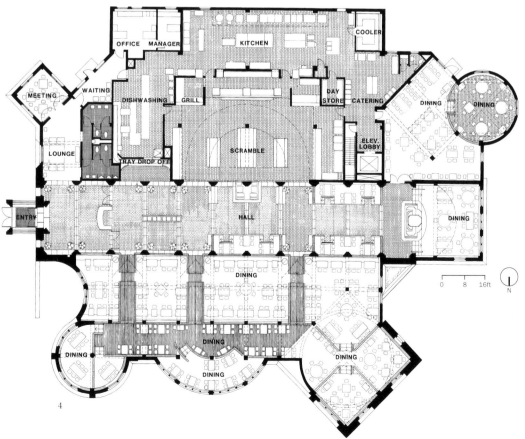

4

6

7

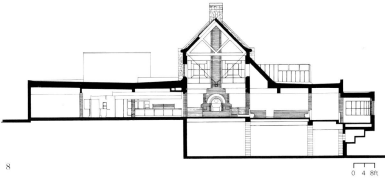

8

0 4 8ft

9

6 Gallery interior
7 Detail of dining area
8 Section
9 Path

Colgate University
Drake Hall

Design/Completion 1992/1995
Hamilton, New York
Colgate University
60,000 square feet/188 rooms
Precast concrete, russet brick, precast voussoirs,
slate roofs, masonry and wood interiors

Through years of observation, teaching, and experience with student groups, we have developed an approach to design that is based on the psychological effects of architecture in student residential settings. Because college students are often self-conscious, their housing should help them overcome their anxiety and connect with their peers in a setting that they see as safe. The housing we have designed at Colgate University observes these principles.

The new dormitory bridges an important pedestrian path between the existing 1950s dormitory (Curtis Hall) and the main dining hall on campus, creating a new quadrangle that serves as an "outdoor living room" where students can socialize.

Drake Hall has bedrooms, lounges, study areas, offices, and a radio station. The lounge, a common room, is adjacent to a single front door so that students may look in, enter, or pass by unselfconsciously. With the main stairway located near the entrance, they must always pass this public realm on the way to their rooms. Circulation throughout the building brings them into contact with each other in public and social areas, allowing for collegial, serendipitous meetings.

A dark russet brick building, Drake Hall harmonizes with other campus buildings. Precast concrete panels form its rusticated base, and giant precast voussoirs frame the semicircular arch, bridging the pedestrian path and enclosing the quadrangle, with views to the campus beyond.

1

2

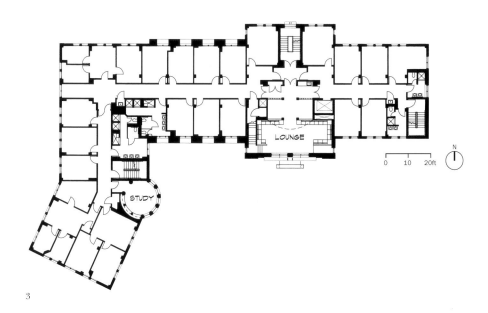

3

1   Site view
2   Entry facade
3   Second floor plan
4   Entrance to stairs and commons

5

6

5 Common lounge
6 Elevation
7 Stair
8 Commons study
9 Bathroom

7

8

9

Colgate University
Curtis Hall

Design/Completion 1992/1995
Hamilton, New York
Colgate University
60,000 square feet
Precast concrete, russet brick, precast voussoirs,
slate roofs, masonry and wood interiors

*A new tower, which combines path, social
spaces, and study spaces, provides an existing
dormitory with amenities that foster a sense
of belonging to a "house."*

While Curtis Hall required renovation,
we also built a new entry tower, adding
common rooms, study areas, and a partial
fifth floor to provide more bedrooms. We
relocated the bathrooms and stairs, and
installed an elevator. In the basement we
constructed new laundry facilities, a game
room, and a health clinic. We replaced the
windows, doors, and structural systems.

The additions to Curtis Hall were clad in
the same materials used in Drake Hall,
with aluminum panels and fins integrated
into the windows to provide sun protection
and a sense of scale. The original yellow
brick cladding was stained to match the
new brick, completing the transformation.

1

2

Before

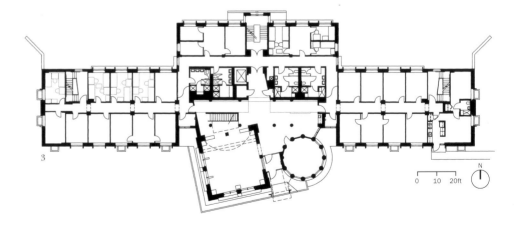

3

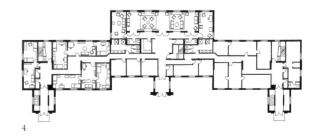

4

1 Entry facade
2 Rear facade
3 First floor plan
4 Floor plan prior to renovation
5 Commons stairwell with study rooms

6

7

8

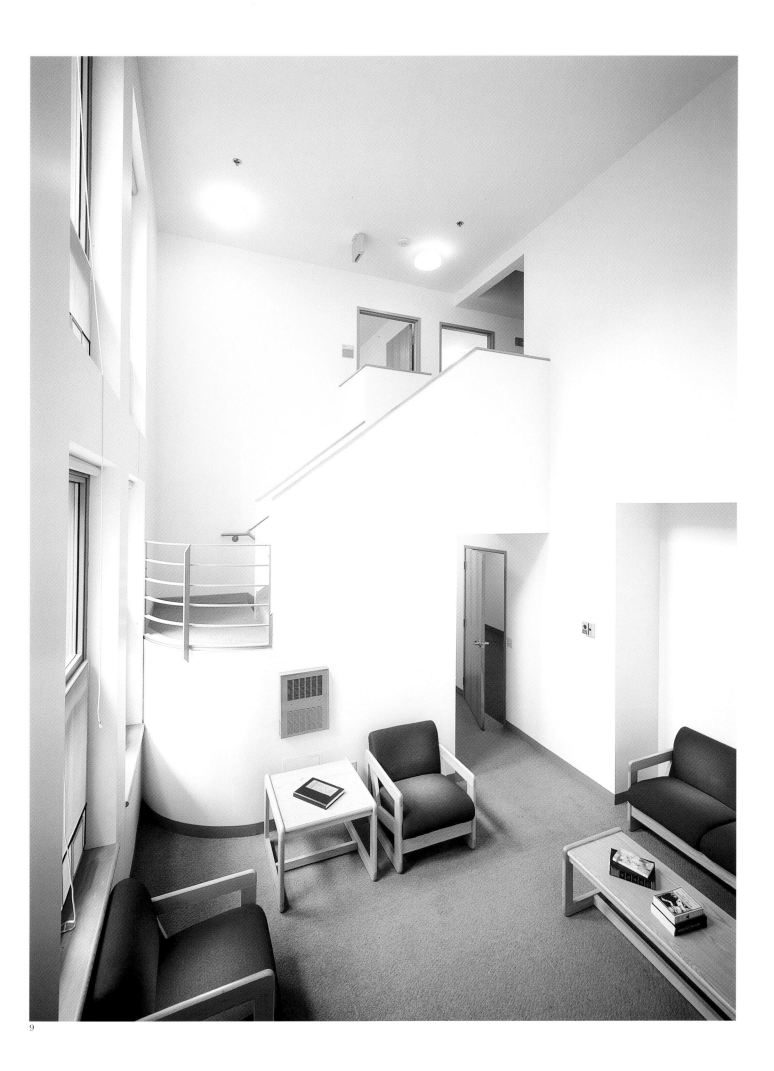

9

University of Rochester Eastman School of Music Student Living Center

Design/Completion 1986/1990
Rochester, New York
University of Rochester
145,000 square feet/350 beds
Steel frame, brick veneer, slate roofs
Brick, limestone, cherry paneling, quarry tile

Continuing our ideas of making communities of dormitories, the design attempts to nurture students by engaging them in interaction with one another through path, portal, entry, and space.

The Eastman School of Music Student Living Center is at the heart of the University of Rochester's cultural center, at Eastman Place facing McKim, Mead and White's Eastman Theater. Home to the students of the music school, it has a dining hall, a small recital hall, common spaces, recreation rooms, student activity rooms, a snack bar, squash courts, and administrative offices.

Derived from the quadrangle style of the collegiate architecture of Oxford, Cambridge and Yale, the Student Living Center has a large central courtyard that acts as an outdoor living room—students can traverse through or choose to linger unselfconsciously. Dormitory rooms in the tower rising above the courtyard are identified with portals, and are clustered into houses arranged vertically.

1   Site plan
2   Tower detail
3   Courtyard
Opposite:
    Tower entry

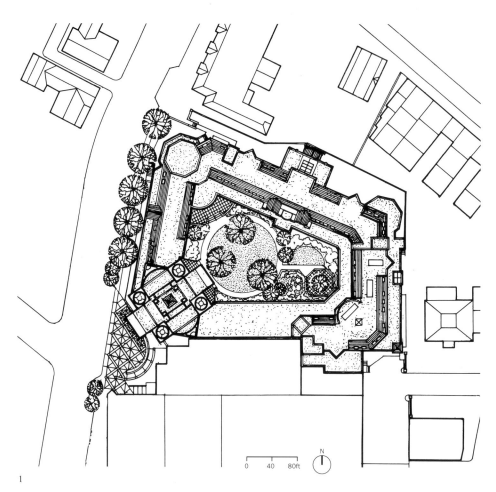

1

0   40   80ft

2

3

5   Ground floor plan
6   Recital room detail
7   Hallway
8   Recital/common room
9   Dining room

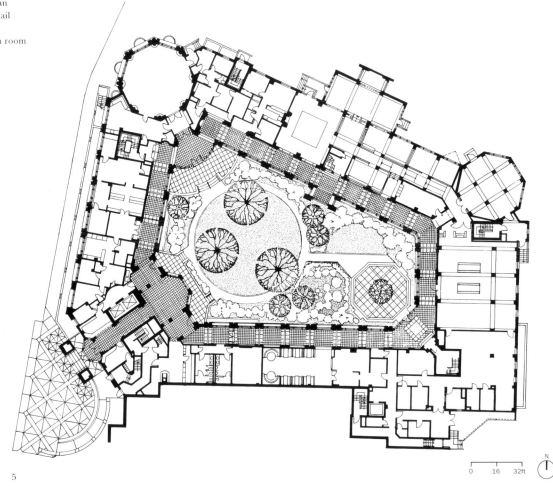

5

0   16   32ft

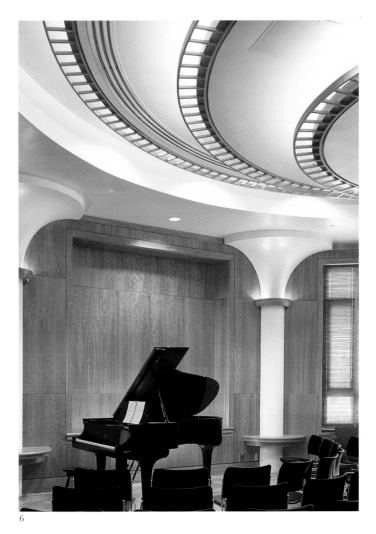

6

7

8

9

Hobart and William Smith Colleges
Scandling Student Center

Design/Completion 1981/1983
Geneva, New York
Hobart and William Smith Colleges
60,000 square feet with a 550-seat dining hall
Steel frame, brick, limestone, slate roofs, wood,
stone and quarry tile floors

*The design mitigates the massive scale
of an existing library that overwhelmed
the sensitive Flemish Revival architecture
of neighboring buildings. Our insertion
acts as a bridge, perceptually linking
these diverse elements and creating a public
outdoor common space within
a new campus precinct by utilizing the
fundamental architectural elements
of structure, hierarchy, light and path.*

Strategically located midway between
a men's campus and a women's campus,
Scandling Student Center is the central
meeting point of Hobart and William
Smith Colleges. It has a multitude of
student uses, including dining spaces,
recreation rooms, seminar rooms, club
facilities, a coffee shop and cafe, study
lounges, student offices, the campus
post office, and a smaller, 150-seat faculty
dining room in the adjacent Humphrey
Building.

Throughout their college years, students
eat most of their meals in the Scandling
Student Center, so it was important to
establish a sense of place with the
character of a sidewalk cafe, where
students are free to see or be seen by
others without feeling self-conscious.

The Center's brick and limestone
exterior recalls the rich Flemish Revival
architecture of the campus. Clerestory
windows and skylights bring natural light
deep into the large spaces, and much of
the large glazing is oriented to the south
to take advantage of sunlight patterns.

1

2

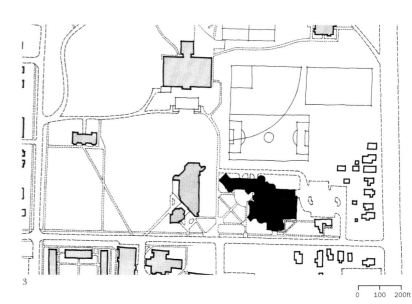

3

1   Building view
2   Courtyard
3   Site plan
Opposite:
    Entry detail

0   100   200ft

6

7

8

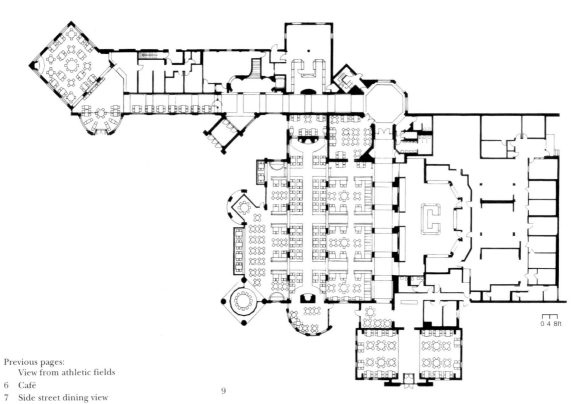

9

Previous pages:
   View from athletic fields
6   Café
7   Side street dining view
8   Faculty dining room
9   Ground floor plan
Opposite:
   Dining room

Alfred University
College of Business and Administration
Franklin W. Olin Building

Design/Completion 1990/1993
Alfred, New York
Alfred University
38,000 square feet
Brick veneer, steel frame
Terra cotta tile roof, aluminum windows, precast
concrete lintel sills and copings, oak veneer
woodwork, quarry tile and carpet

*The design strengthens the continuity and
unity of the Alfred campus while respectfully
proposing a new direction. The building
represents the college through path and space,
bringing faculty and students together in
corridors as well as classrooms. Main entries on
two levels and a central, open stair hall with a
double-story commons act as a vertical street to
knit together the building's pathways.*

The commons opens to the main internal
path, acting as a central breakout space for
students on the two main classroom
floors. Wide circulation spaces and
lobbies at each level, glazing at entries
into classrooms, and the clustering of
faculty offices around a skylit work space
further support openness, accessibility,
and interchange.

The building has state-of-the-art seminar
rooms, lecture halls, case-study classrooms,
and faculty offices, a behavior laboratory
for the study of human interaction, and
a center for computer management
systems training.

The use of brick provides a warm and
lively sensibility, enhanced through the
use of garden gates, a conference room
that overlooks the major growth corridor
of the campus, and chimney forms that
enclose ventilators. The symmetrical
massing, sloping roofs, and exterior
materials reinforce the continuity of the
campus architecture, both old and new.

1

2

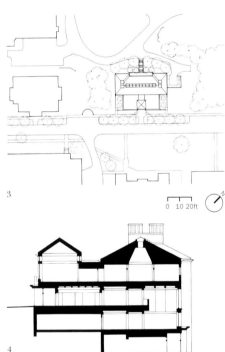

3

0 10 20ft

4

0 4 8ft

1 Entry facade
2 View of entry
3 Site plan
4 Section
Following pages:
   View looking southwest

6

7

8

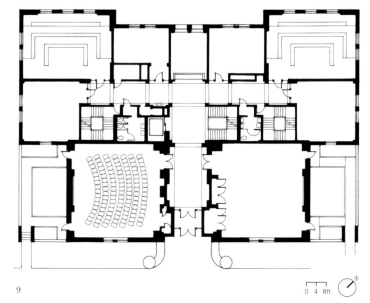

9

6 Entry hall
7 Second floor administration offices
8 First floor meeting space
9 Third floor plan
10 Second floor conference room

Alfred University, College of Business and Administration, Franklin W. Olin Building   61

Northeastern University Law School
Kariotis Hall

Design/Completion 1980/1983
Boston, Massachusetts
Northeastern University
30,000 square feet (new)
80,000 square feet (renovated)
Concrete foundation and columns supporting
cast-in-place waffle slab; waterproof membrane
under a pedestrian plaza; brick veneer masonry

*We were intrigued by the idea of making
Kariotis Hall bridge the gap in style between its
nineteenth century neighbors: mercantile
buildings and the sober modern buildings of the
university's southern campus. As winners of an
invited planning and architectural competition
for the Law School, we produced a master plan
for the South Campus, where it resides amid
neighborhood buildings of Boston.*

A new classroom building, Kariotis Hall,
is at the cusp of the master plan,
restructuring a point of confluence that
is now a gateway to the campus. Through
its masonry architecture, the four-story
building attempts to knit neighboring
buildings, including one nineteenth
century brick commercial building, into
the fabric of the campus and the new
architecture of the Law School Plaza.
Brickwork, projecting cornice forms,
glass, slate, and ashlar concrete emphasize
the complexity of these relationships,
while red brick masonry and the projected
curve forms of the lobbies and stair tower
recall the bay windows of the surrounding
Back Bay neighborhood.

We renovated the Law Library and linked
it to the new classroom building,
dramatically increasing the Law School's
classroom space. Most of the classrooms,
lecture halls, and offices in Kariotis Hall
are located below the new Law School
Plaza to preserve precious open space.
Sunken courtyards provide daylight to
the below-grade spaces. Kariotis Hall
celebrates the entry to the new Law
School Plaza and acts as a gateway to
the South Campus.

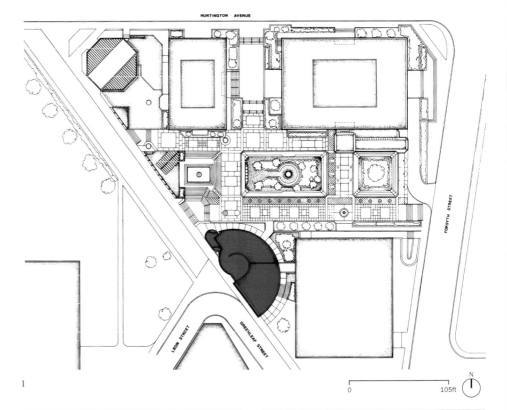

1

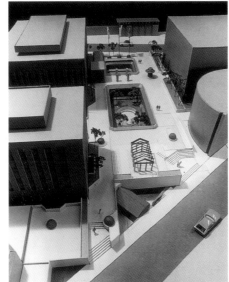

2

3

1   Site plan
2   Model
3   Plaza
4   Entry facade
5   Ground floor plan

4

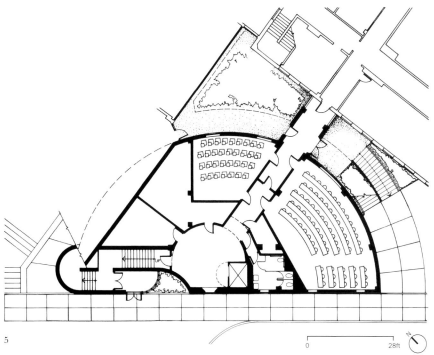

5

0   28ft

N

6

7

8

6   Entry facade at twilight
7   Lecture hall
8   Stair detail
9   View from street

9

Dartmouth College
East Wheelock Residential Cluster

Design/Completion 1983/1987
Hanover, New Hampshire
100,000 square feet/240 beds
Light-gauge and conventional steel framing,
brick veneer, copper roofs, aluminum windows,
concrete plaza and walks
Painted sheetrock, ceramic tile,
wood millwork and trim

*Fraternity houses were traditionally the most
popular form of housing at Dartmouth College,
which was until recently a male-only university.
Our design provides an inviting residential
alternative to the fraternity house by breaking
the scale of a dormitory into "houses" with
individual living rooms, central stairways, and
study/seminar rooms. Built into a hillside, the
three buildings join at a common ground floor
that creates an informal quadrangle—an
outdoor living room.*

The residential buildings are a prototype
for Dartmouth's innovative "cluster"
concept, integrating housing with a
variety of places for study and socializing
to enhance student life and facilitate
neighborly connections.

Following the Dartmouth pattern of
a village of related buildings, the cluster
is composed of three informally grouped
buildings, each housing 80 students.
Each building has a gable-roofed center
with a double-height living room, study
rooms and a common stairway. On either
side, four-story wings house the student
suites and single rooms. The corridors end
in small seating areas with bay windows.

The Cluster Common, a one-story building
partially below grade, is a meeting area
that connects all three buildings. Above
it a small plaza serves as an informal
meeting place. The design fosters
human interaction via entries, pathways,
and gathering places that give students
the freedom to socialize or find a quiet
place to study.

Red bricks, sharply pitched roofs, dormers,
and the occasional oculus tie the new
buildings to older Georgian buildings
on the campus. In the summer, the
residential cluster provides the same uses
for guests attending the College's summer
conference programs.

1   Site plan
2   Courtyard
3   View of Building A
4   Plaza plan
5   Building A floor plan
6   Building B floor plan
7   Building C floor plan

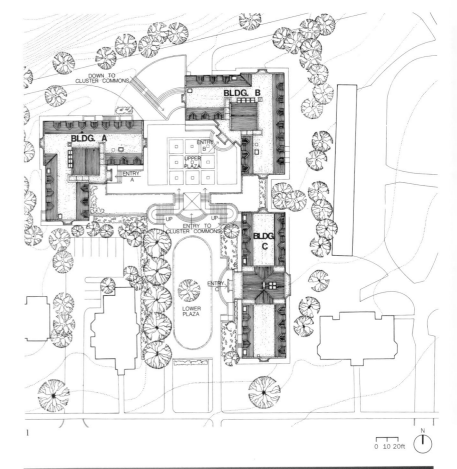

1

2

3

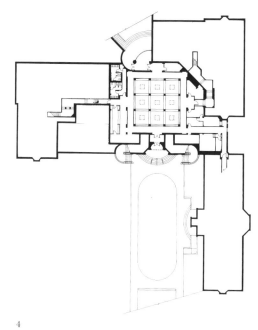

4

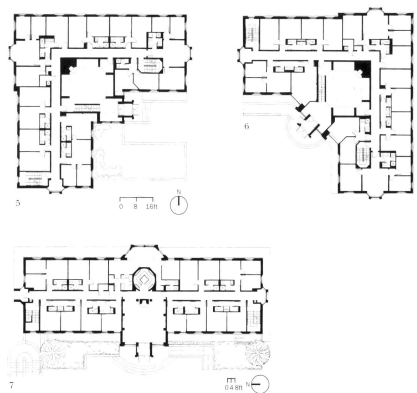

5

6

7

0 8 16ft N

0 4 8ft N

8

9

10

11

12

13

8   Building B, view of entry to common room
9   North entry to common room
10   View of common room
11   Residence hall entry
12   Fourth floor residence hall room
13   Living room suite

University of Connecticut
Northwest Quadrangle
Dining Hall and Dormitories

Design/Completion 1998/2000
Storrs, Connecticut
University of Connecticut
27,000 square feet
Brick, curved lead-coated copper roof forms,
aluminum frame windows, ceramic tile,
sliding wood screens, luminaires

*We are attempting to renew six residence halls to
enhance the quality of life for freshman students
at this state university. A new seventh building
will be a dining hall, and will be conceived as
a place with great spatial variety, ornamented
with changing natural light to allow for a
continual sense of discovery and renewal.*

The Northwest Quadrangle consists
of seven postwar dormitories that serve
as freshman housing. The program calls
for reconfiguration of the quadrangle into
an integrated coeducational residential
complex. A new dining hall will replace
one of the existing dormitories, and the
ground floors of the remaining six will be
redesigned to accommodate an expanded
program for student residential life.

The two-story dining hall will seat 550
students at ground level, and will have
meeting rooms and a lecture hall on the
second floor. The scope of renovation to
the six dormitories will include the
comprehensive replacement of building
infrastructure systems, modernization of
data/telecom systems, new sprinklers,
and full accessibility modifications. Two
of the dormitories will contain quad-wide
services including administrative quarters,
computer laboratories, a mailroom, and
recreational spaces.

Landscape architecture will include the
construction of an outdoor amphitheater,
new pathways, and the planting of trees
to create a wooded setting for the building
group.

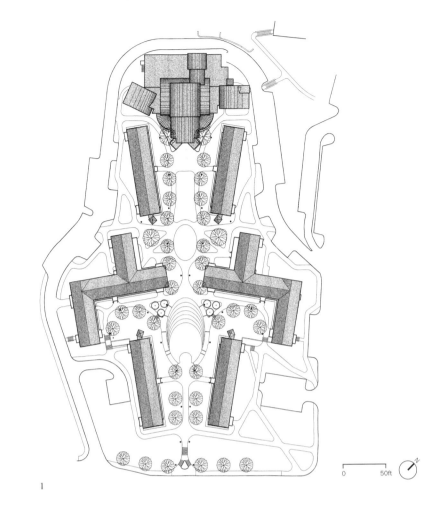

1

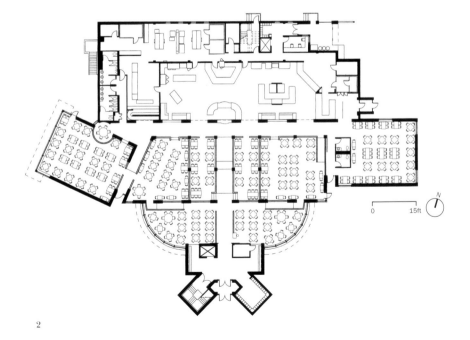

2

1   Site plan
2   Ground floor plan
3   Entry elevation, computer rendering
4   Entry elevation
5   Section

3

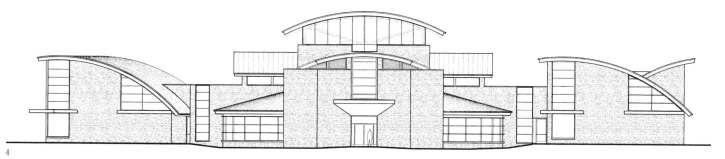

4

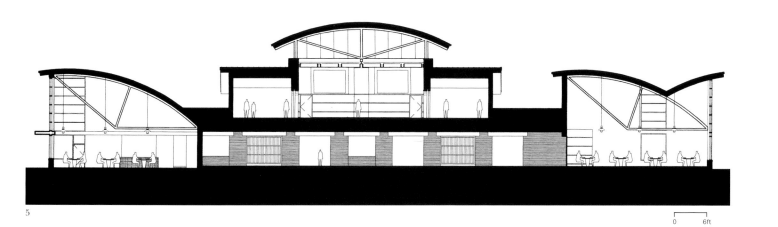

5

0   6ft

Western Connecticut State University Residential Village

Design/Completion 1996/1999
Danbury, Connecticut
Connecticut State University System
180,000 square feet
Reinforced masonry walls, precast concrete
plank floors and roof, concrete masonry walls

*This residence hall expresses many of
the design ideas and principles we have
developed for residential life: a single main
entry, a stairway and commons off the entry,
and spaces broken into recognizable
neighborhoods or "houses."*

This 425-bed dormitory is massed in
segmental "houses" along the brow of
a hill in a crescent following a main road.
This scheme reinforces the central campus
pathway, which links the road to the
classroom building; the field house on a
wooded knoll to the north of the road is
similarly reinforced as a campus landmark.

The siting of the building takes advantage
of uninterrupted views to the countryside,
while also optimizing sunlight to the
residential units. Sixty-five percent of
the suites face this direction. The main
building lounge or "commons" is sited
with a large terrace facing southwest.

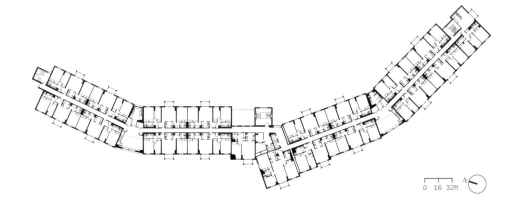

1

1   Ground floor plan
2   Rear view with balconies
3   View of residence hall
4   Site plan
5   Side elevation

2

3

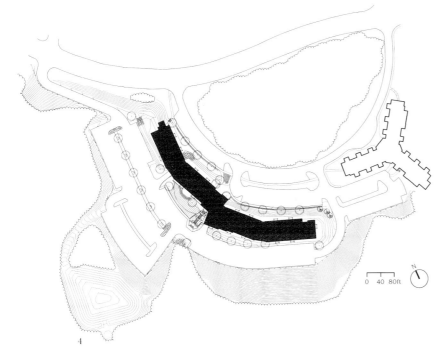

4

5

University of Connecticut
C.E. Waring Hall

Design/Completion 1998/2000
Storrs, Connecticut
University of Connecticut
80,000 square feet
Steel frame, masonry wall

The design attempts to renew and transform an existing 1959 chemistry building into the new home of the College of Liberal Arts and Sciences, in which five academic departments will be consolidated into one building. The focal point of the design is a new entry tower and four-story stair hall oriented toward the central campus pedestrian path. The imagery of the glazed tower asserts the importance of the building's new uses, while providing a solution to the functional challenges of entering at a mid-level between the ground and first floor.

The renovation is confined to approximately 80,000 square feet contained in an existing "U" shape of the building, which houses the Chemistry Department laboratories, classrooms and faculty offices. The Hall requires extensive renewal of the exterior envelope to address deferred maintenance concerns, including new roofing, window replacement, and masonry repair. Renovation of the interior includes reconfiguring the spaces for their new uses, and replacing the mechanical, electrical, telecommunication, and life safety building systems.

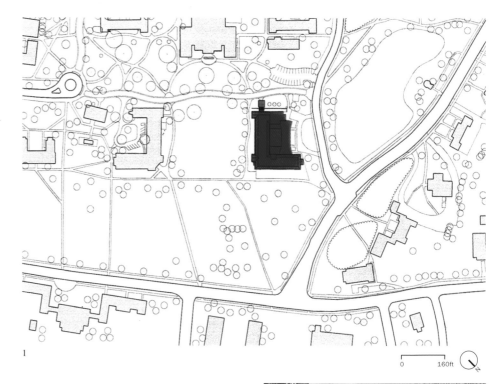

1

0   160ft

Before

1   Site rendering
2   Computer rendering of entry elevation
3   First floor plan

2

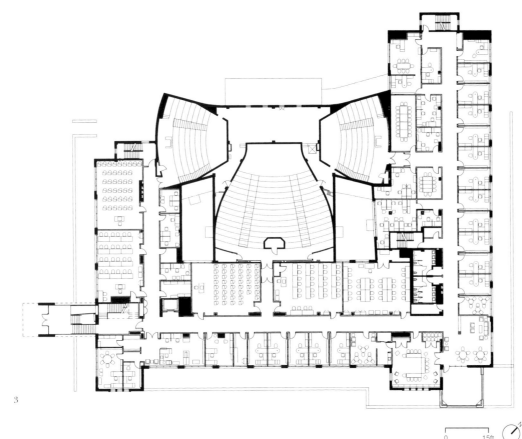

3

0   15ft

Yale University
School of Organization
and Management
Donaldson Commons

Design/Completion 1977/1980
New Haven, Connecticut
General Instrument Corporation
10,000 square feet
Red brick, aluminum and glass,
precast concrete lintels

Our design of Donaldson Commons attempts to expand the capacity of modern architecture to encompass intimacy, warmth, charm, and historical continuity—most notably the tradition of the Yale College system, in which the interior courtyard becomes the dominant void and the buildings act as walls of enclosure.

Our approach reflects principles we have developed through our experience on college campuses, which are based on the psychological effects of experiencing architecture in academic settings.

The notion of the unselfconsciousness of a sidewalk cafe contributed to the creation of a benign setting in which students can observe each other, socialize, or choose to be alone. The clear ordering of spaces allows them to proceed from one main entry to a common hall or "street" which provides choices of dining spaces.

A variety of dining areas offers various choices: a communal refectory, smaller dining rooms, and bay window alcoves. Because the average human head is 8 inches high, the design utilizes 8-inch tiers to enable students to see each other across a large space. This fosters a sense of both casual contact and intimacy.

The scale of the building respects the scale of the neighborhood. The use of natural materials gives the commons durability that has allowed it to age gracefully. The 350-seat dining hall resulted from the remodeling of a 100-seat dining hall that was formerly a divinity school chapel, and the addition of a new wing.

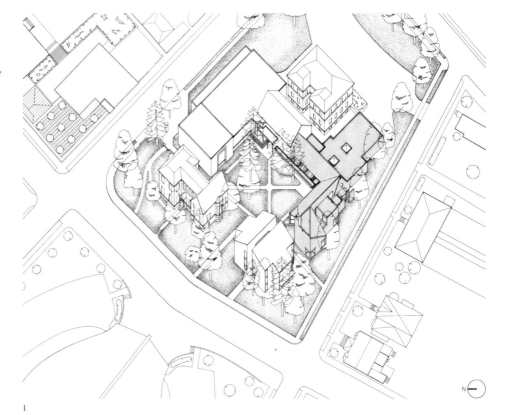

1

N

2

1   Site rendering
2   Entry court
3   Side elevation
4&5   Sections
6   Side elevation

3

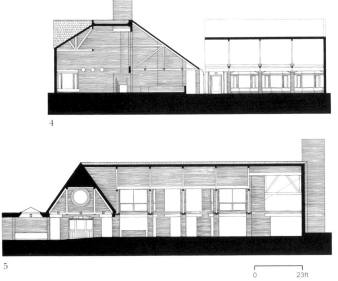

4

5

0   23ft

6

7

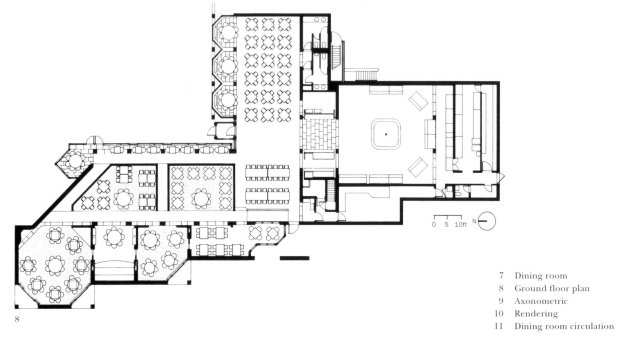

8

7 Dining room
8 Ground floor plan
9 Axonometric
10 Rendering
11 Dining room circulation

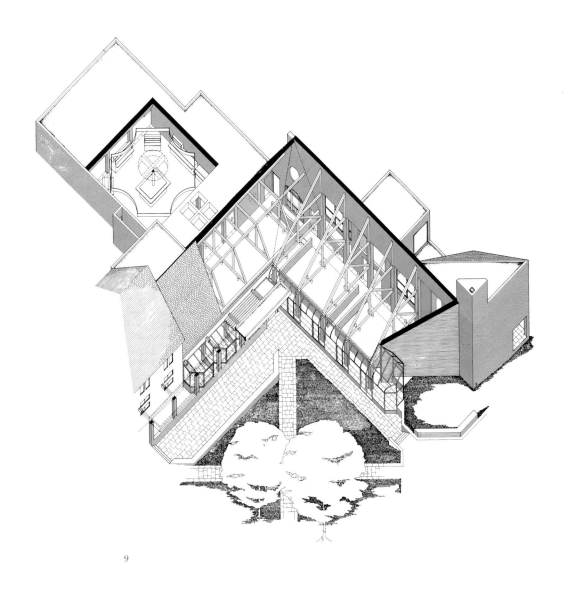

9

10

11

Yale University
Sterling Law School, Library and Lecture Hall

Design/Completion 1976/1978
New Haven, Connecticut
Yale University
5,000 square feet
Oak furniture, painted plaster walls

One of the most elegant interior spaces on campus, the Yale Law School Library was designed by James Gamble Rogers in 1932. However, by the late 1970s the library had grown shabby, overcrowded, and noisy with the influx of copying machines. In addition, one of the lecture halls at the school put students at an awkward distance from the speaker. The Law School asked us to make both of these spaces more amenable.

We restored the shell of the library and its rich detailing, shifted the photocopiers to adjacent areas, and replaced most of the reading tables with oak carrels and comfortable chairs. We relocated the card catalogue to the center of the room for better visibility and access. The new design of the carrels provides task lighting, while up-lighting enhances the lovely restored painted wood ceiling beams and gargoyle capitals.

We reoriented the lecture hall, placing the speaker in the center of the long wall, which improved both the visual and acoustical relationships. Seating is along new stepped and curved platforms. Many elements of the old room were retained, including the handsome oak wainscotting and doors. New elements include dropped beams that conceal the lighting, and new furnishings.

1

Before

Before

1 Lecture hall
Opposite:
   Library

Yale University
Calhoun College

Design/Completion 1988/1989
New Haven, Connecticut
Yale University
140,000 square feet
Ornamental stone and metal,
wood paneling and trim

The design solution focused on preservation. Where new architectural interventions were needed, the intent was to envision the building in the eyes of its architect, and to preserve and enhance the original architecture.

Calhoun College, built in 1932, was designed in the collegiate Gothic style by John Russell Pope. It housed student residential suites, a dining hall, studies, recreation and common rooms, faculty apartments, and a master's house. Originally designed for 120 students, over the years its population grew to approximately 240. After more than 56 years of use, overcrowding had robbed the suites of their original generosity, and cafeteria service had been shoehorned into the former serving kitchen. Common spaces were also inadequate and the basement had been adapted into a series of makeshift spaces for recreation, music, theater, and crafts.

The program called for extensive suite reconfigurations, including the full redesign of the east wing. In the kitchen renovation, the basement area has been fully modernized, allowing many first floor operations to move downstairs. The first floor servery has been enlarged, and the dining hall has been restored.

The basement has undergone many changes to improve the organization of its various spaces and to provide more appropriate design for these spaces, including a lobby, a performance hall, and various activity rooms.

By discreetly replacing all plumbing, heating, and electrical systems, and installing new sprinklers, alarms, and security systems, the master's house, faculty apartments, and library were restored, as were Calhoun's slate roof and stone and brick facade.

1

2

3

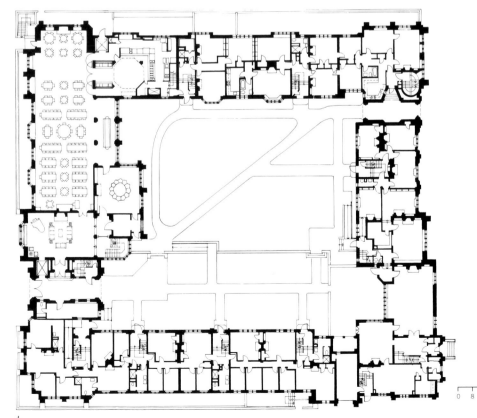

4

1   Courtyard
2   Common room
3   Dining room
4   Ground floor plan

0   8 16ft   N

Yale University
Old Campus Dormitories

Design/Completion 1975/1978
New Haven, Connecticut
Yale University
215,000 square feet
Masonry load-bearing walls, slate roofs, plaster

The designs preserve the existing architecture of the old campus and reduce overcrowding through the use of "found" space in attics and basements. We transformed existing "double-decker" bedrooms and barracks-style floor plans into six-person suites with their own bathrooms, living rooms, and sitting rooms, helping to create a sense of responsibility for students in maintaining their own living spaces.

The Old Campus dormitories of Yale University, which date back to the mid-nineteenth century, comprise six of the oldest buildings on campus, and represent a symbolic gateway to undergraduate education at the university. By the late 1970s they were outdated, unsafe, overcrowded and in need of renovation. We collaborated with Edward Larabee Barnes to perform modifications and upgrades while preserving and enhancing their unique architectural character, both inside and out.

Our goal was to set design objectives and standards that would take existing conditions and adapt them without making any noticeable changes to the interior. The new programs for Lawrance, Welch, Farnam, Vanderbilt, Durfee and McClellan Halls called for full suite reconfiguration, fully replacing the plumbing, heating, and electrical systems, installing new sprinklers, modifying life safety egress, and restoring the buildings' exteriors. In addition, we adapted sloping ceilings and gabled roofs into skylit rooms with an open studio effect, and introduced windows to provide ventilation and natural light in all rooms.

The reconfigured dormitories provide students with privacy, spatial variety, and a gain of 120 beds overall, without any noticeable changes to the architectural integrity of Yale's historic Old Campus buildings.

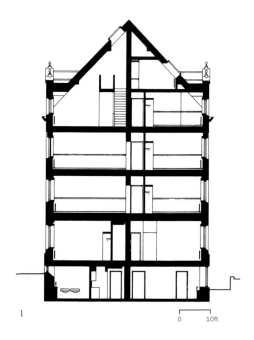

1

0   10ft

2

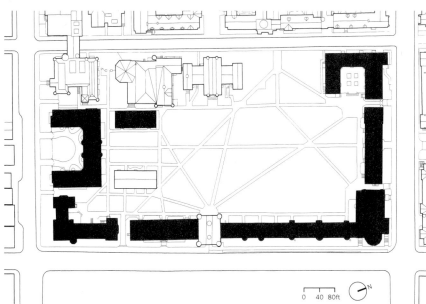

1 Welch Hall section
2 College Street facade
3 Site plan
Opposite:
   Living room, Welch Hall

3

0   40 80ft

N

Yale University
Bingham Hall

Design/Completion 1995/1997
New Haven, Connecticut
Yale University
62,000 square feet
Steel, concrete, plaster

*Because of additional housing needs,
an unused attic space was converted to
a new residential floor. We added circular
windows to bring light to this floor.*

Bingham Hall, on Yale University's Old
Campus, was constructed in 1928 and
contains faculty offices, seminar rooms,
a library, and six floors of residential
suites. The vacant ninth floor, originally
designed to house an observatory, was
converted to new student living quarters.
This enabled the university, which is always
in need of more residential space on its
campus, to house more students at the
heart of Yale College.

We also made Bingham Hall fully
accessible to the disabled by enlarging
and extending the elevator to serve all
floors. We redesigned the basement
spaces to create new offices for the
University Chaplain and her staff.

Most of the deteriorated exterior cast
stone gargoyles were replaced, as were
the windows and roof. Interior renovations
were comprehensive and included a
complete replacement of the building
systems infrastructure and reconfiguration
of the student suites.

We designed the renovations so that
construction work could take place in
two phases while the building remained
in use.

1

Before

Before

1 Top floor addition interior
Opposite:
    Exterior

Schools

The Greenwich Academy
Wallace Performing Arts Center,
New Athletic Center
and Gymnasium Renovation

Design/Completion 1994/1998
Greenwich, Connecticut
The Greenwich Academy
26,500 square feet (Performing Arts Center)
28,000 square feet (Athletic Center including
Gymnasium Renovation)

*The setting is a lovely residential neighborhood
of large, early twentieth century houses. One of
these, Campbell Hall, now an admissions and
administrative building for the Greenwich
Academy, has a dominant, well-proportioned,
classical portico. It anchors the remaining
academic buildings, which are effectively hidden
behind brick walls.*

Our work at the Greenwich Academy,
a college-preparatory school for girls,
involved designing buildings to advance
the school's arts and athletic programs,
while complementing its existing
architecture. In doing so, we also designed
a new garden courtyard providing better
overall access to the campus.

The centerpiece of the Performing Arts
Center is a 400-seat theater. An intimate
setting for youthful performers, it has a
shallow raked floor and a low balcony.
The Center includes a smaller, 100-seat
flexible theater, dance, choral and
instrumental practice areas, and theater
support spaces. The theater lobby is an
art gallery with a partially enclosed path
leading to a neighboring boys' school
that shares classes with the Academy.
These welcoming indoor spaces are
served by multiple access routes, allowing
for learning to be enhanced by the
serendipitous meeting of students,
faculty and staff.

The Athletic Center has a new double
gymnasium with five squash courts, a fitness
room, and locker and shower facilities.
We also expanded and renovated the
existing Ramsing Gymnasium, restoring its
first floor entrance and adding a new two-
level lobby that provides entry from the
garden courtyard and athletic fields. From
the lobby, viewers can look into the new
gymnasium and the fields beyond.

1   Entry drive

1

2

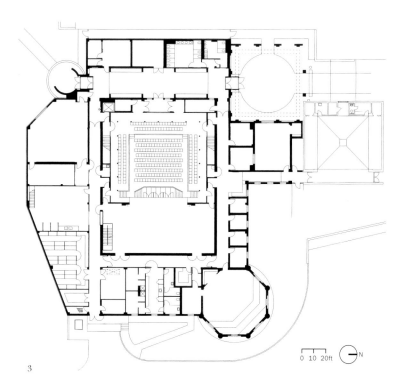

0 10 20ft   N

3

4

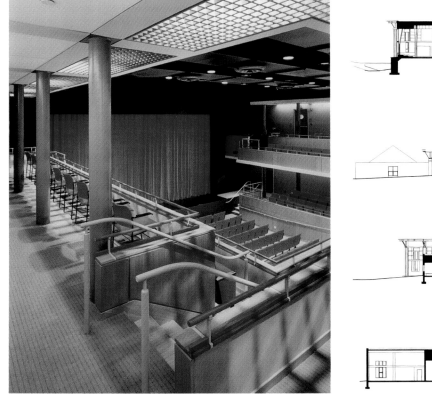

5

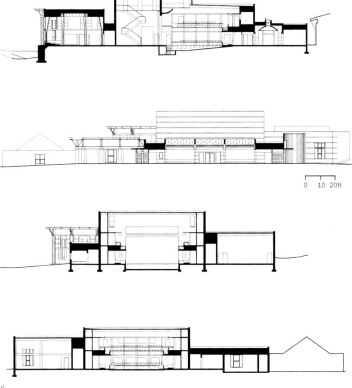

6

7

8

9

10

11

12

13

14

Taft School
Arts and Humanities Building

Design/Completion 1983/1986
Watertown, Connecticut
Taft School
42,000 square feet
Exposed brick, cruciform mullions,
natural finish oak, quarry tile

In the renovation and expansion of this building, we explored the development of an appropriate new architectural language that offered continuity and authenticity without pastiche.

Our task was to convert two unused gymnasia into a new Arts and Humanities Wing for the Taft School and visually unite it with surrounding buildings, including one four-story collegiate Gothic building designed by Cram, Goodhue and Ferguson, and later enhanced by James Gamble Rogers. Loosely grouped around a pond, the buildings lacked focus. Our transformation made the pond the focal point of a new campus center, anchoring the surrounding architecture.

We utilized forms and details that derive from the Gothic vocabulary of the surrounding buildings, including new gabled stair towers marking the entries, matching water-struck brick, a gabled slate roof with blind dormers, and windows with cast stone details and cruciform mullions. An octagonal corner tower is now the hub of the student union's brick paved terrace cafe.

The volume inside the older of the former gyms provided high spaces for the 200-seat experimental black box theater and a dance studio, while volume in the newer gym allowed for construction of an upper level. The new wing provides additional educational and cultural spaces including classrooms, seminar rooms, faculty offices, visual arts studios, music rooms, and film studios.

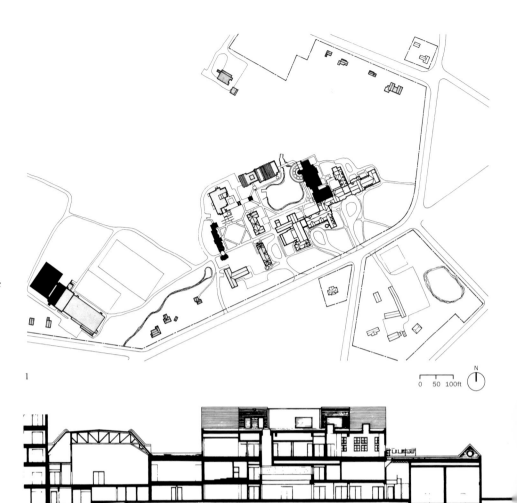

1 Site plan
2 Section
3 Art classroom
4 Exterior detail
5 Entry elevation
6 Ground floor plan

5

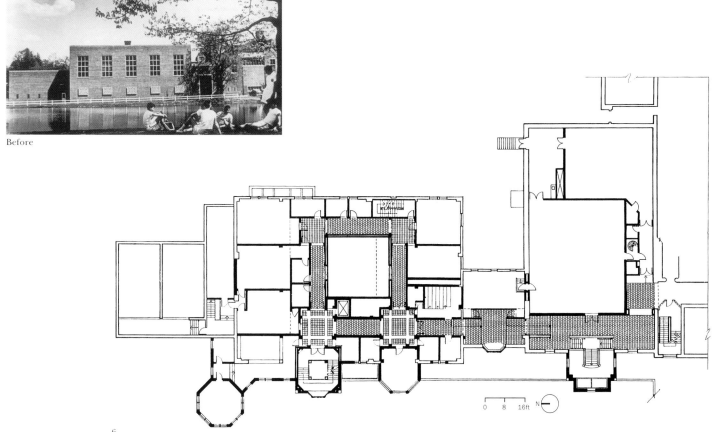

Before

6

Taft School
Residence Hall

Design/Completion 1987/1989
Watertown, Connecticut
20,000 square feet
Steel frame with brick veneer, precast concrete,
slate roof, exposed brick interiors

This project is a continuation of the Taft experiment: transitional rather than stylistic purity. The success of this idea depends not on theory, but on how well it can be implemented.

The residence hall maintains and enhances the vernacular of the collegiate Gothic campus. Bay windows, fenestration, dormers, interwoven brickwork, and cast stone detailing unify its interior and exterior. Its arch acts as a gateway over an important pedestrian path leading from the academic and residential campuses to the playing fields. Sited together with the school's library and three dormitories designed by James Gamble Rogers, the building forms a new campus quadrangle.

With 12 double rooms and 17 single rooms, the three-story residence hall provides coeducational housing for 41 upperclassmen. Student rooms are arranged in singles and doubles off north and south central corridors, with a major entry and stair tower at the center of the east facade. Each floor is equipped with laundry, toilet, and support facilities including TV/recreation rooms.

Above the arch is a library for informal study. The faculty residences at the end of each floor are architecturally distinct from the dormitories by virtue of their scale and major access, but are connected to provide social and supervisory circulation. Each faculty residence has its own formal entry, three bedrooms, and living, dining, and study rooms.

1

1   Stairwell detail
2   Faculty house elevation
3   Entry elevation
4   Second floor plan
5   First floor plan

2

3

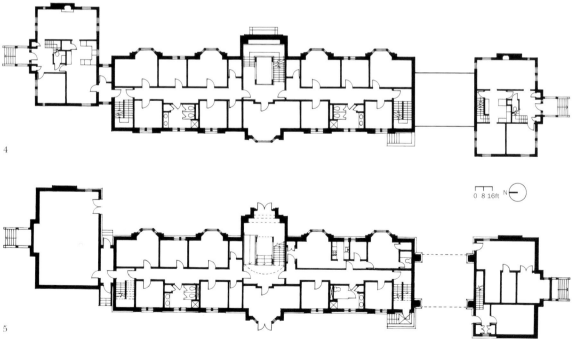

4

5

0 8 16ft   N

Lyme Academy of Fine Arts
Master Plan

Design/Completion 1999/2001
Old Lyme, Connecticut
Lyme Academy of Fine Arts
65 acres

The Lyme Academy of Fine Arts is a small college for the visual arts located on the main street of Old Lyme, Connecticut, a lovely New England village and home to the American Impressionist school of painting. The Academy has earned a national reputation for a curriculum of study focused on the classical disciplines in drawing, painting and sculpture. The success and public recognition of the Academy have generated increased enrollment pressures and a subsequent need to grow.

We have developed a master plan for growth that envisions a new campus integrated into the fabric of its village setting. To its current building complex— an eighteenth century house with various renovated outbuildings and additions— the Academy will add buildings for studios, classrooms, administrative and social uses, and public galleries. Projected long-range plans include housing for resident artists and graduate students.

The master plan proposes to make places, portals, and paths that take advantage of the native meadow, woodland, and riverfront settings, while addressing the Old Lyme Historic District streetfront with contextually appropriate and residentially scaled "houses." The garden and meadow spaces behind the houses become settings for plein-air painting, sculpture, and social and recreational activities. Woodland areas are reached via a new road that winds along the topography to open up precincts for residential clusters, fields and ponds.

1   Site rendering
2   Site plan

1

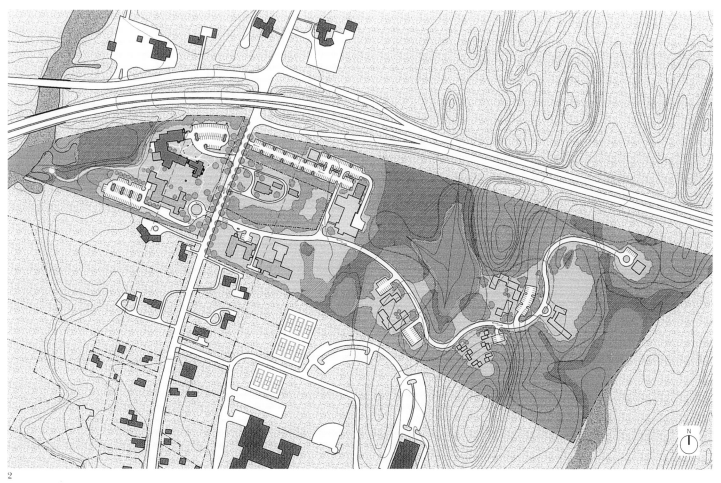

2

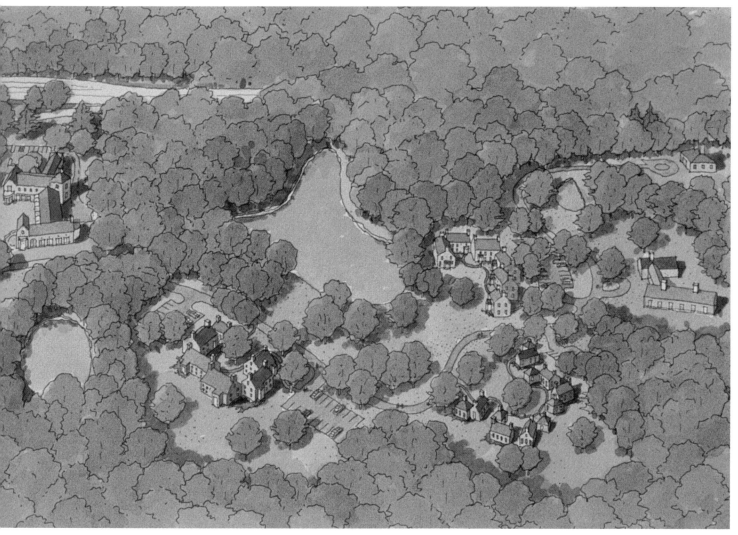

William H. Hall High School

Design/Completion 1997/1999
West Hartford, Connecticut
William H. Hall High School
20,000 square feet (new);
250,000 square feet (renovated)
Steel frame, brick veneer, lead-coated copper
roof copings, aluminum windows,
exposed structure classrooms

Our design attempts to energize a slumbering academic building and evoke an air of excitement about learning. The addition is visible upon entering the site and creates a foil for the truncated massing of the existing school, allowing one to appreciate the whole complex in a new way.

Built in 1970, William H. Hall High School reflects many of the approaches common in school design of that period: exterior walls were built without windows to cut energy costs, while the use of deep floor plates left large areas lacking natural light or ventilation.

We reorganized the existing building to meet the needs of a changing curriculum and a projected enrollment increase from 1,200 to 1,500 students. The library is now larger. Non-academic and administrative rooms were relocated to permit academic spaces to expand in distinct disciplinary neighborhoods. We increased the amount of circulation space and reorganized it to reduce congestion and improve the flow of students between classes.

We added windows throughout the building. Interior spaces that had no natural light have been converted to support spaces that do not need to be used for extended periods. We also relocated many offices and teaching areas to the building perimeter and provided them with windows.

The addition has three levels: art and technology studios are on the ground level; general-purpose classrooms and science laboratories are on the two floors above.

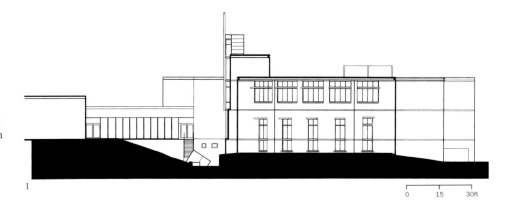

1

0   15   30ft

2

1   Building elevation
2   Computer rendering
3   Construction view
4   Ground floor plan

3

4

0 15 30ft

N

West Hills/Conte School

Design/Completion 1998/1999
New Haven, Connecticut
State of Connecticut
100,000 square feet
Brick, aluminum-frame curtain walls and
aluminum sunscreen panels, lead-coated
copper roof projection, built-up roofing

The design is an attempt to connect the
Italianate past of the Wooster Square
neighborhood to a 1961 Skidmore, Owings
& Merrill "temples in a field" school—with
a smile and a wink, and excitement about
learning.

The existing school consists of two
buildings: a main two-story building with
classrooms, offices, pool, and gymnasium
surrounding a central courtyard; and a
separate 250-seat auditorium building.
The buildings are flat-roofed with precast
exterior concrete wall panels and floor-to-
ceiling curtain wall systems. Regularly
spaced exterior concrete columns form
a perimeter colonnade on all sides of the
existing buildings. Our design renovates
and expands the school to serve children
from ages five through fourteen.

A two-story addition between the existing
classroom building and auditorium
includes classrooms, a stair tower, a
new entrance, and a covered connection
between the auditorium and the classroom
building. A second single-story addition to
the south of the existing building provides
additional classrooms, administration
offices, and a second entrance. The
exterior walls are brick, with metal panel
and curtain wall infill.

1

1 East elevation computer rendering
2 Site plan
3 Building plan
Following pages:
    Entry detail computer rendering

Before

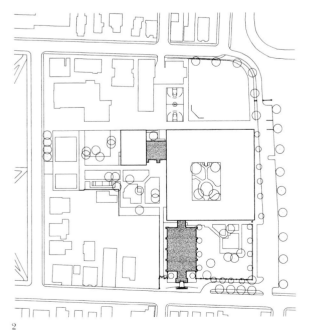

2

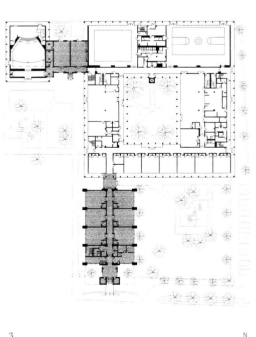

3

0   50ft   N

Conard High School

Design/Completion 1996/1999
West Hartford, Connecticut
Conard High School
50,000 square feet (new); 220,000 square feet (renovated)
Steel frame, brick, built-up roof
Painted aluminum panels, aluminum windows, carpet, vinyl and ceramic tile floors

The renovation and expansion of Conard High School restores civic pride and excitement to what was a tired, worn warehouse of a school. The original school, built in 1957 with a technology wing added in 1977, had numerous deficiencies, was badly in need of repair, and required expansion to accommodate increased student enrollments. It was a complicated building with many deficiencies related to life safety and accessibility to be resolved.

The Conard school administration had an ambitious project schedule, requiring the completion of design and construction in three years, while the school remained open. We developed cost-effective design solutions that equipped the school with state-of-the-art technology, enabling energy-conserving systems to be installed, and we improved learning spaces.

Our work included a new gymnasium and athletic facilities, a new library and media center, new classrooms and science laboratories, and administrative guidance and student services offices.

1

1 Entry facade
2 Entry detail
3 Plan

2

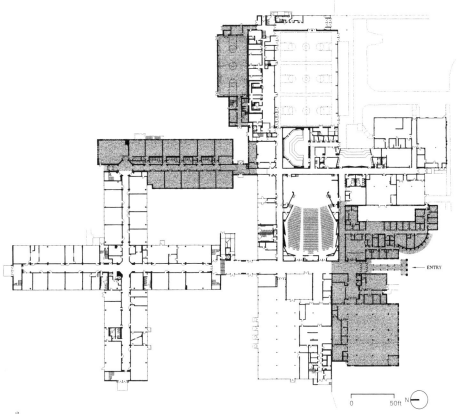

3

Institutional/Corporate/Commercial

The Pocantico Conference Center
of the Rockefeller Brothers Fund

Design/Completion 1991/1995
Tarrytown, New York
The Rockefeller Brothers Fund
20,000 square feet
New steel plate entry vestibule and courtyard bay,
wood replacement windows, plaster, white oak,
cherry paneling and trim, metal laminate paneling,
nylon fabric

In 1979, the Rockefeller family
bequeathed 84 acres of its estate to the
National Trust for Historic Preservation
for use as a museum and conference
center to advance the philanthropic
mission of the Rockefeller Brothers Fund.
The property includes the family house,
Kykuit, built in 1909 and 1913; the
Orangerie of 1908; and the Coach Barn of
1902 and 1913.

Our work involved two phases: restoring
Kykuit to serve as a museum of the family's
history and to provide guest rooms for
conferees; and renovating the Coach Barn
into a state-of-the-art international
conference center with guest rooms.

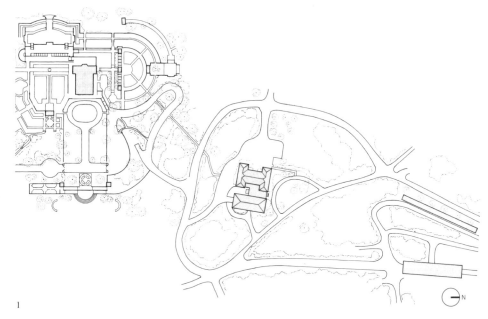

1

2

3

1   Site plan of Kykuit and the Coach Barn
2   Entrance to the Coach Barn
3   Outdoor plaza, Coach Barn
Opposite:
    New entry portal, Coach Barn

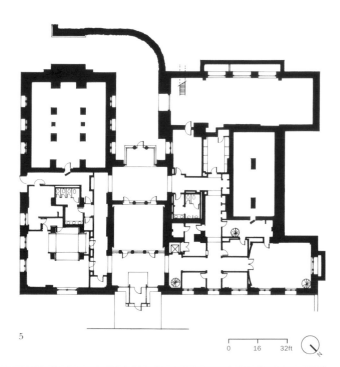

The Coach Barn

Originally a three-story utility building with horse stables, an automobile garage, a workshop, and various maintenance and staff rooms, the Coach Barn is now the Rockefeller Brothers Fund's international conference center.

We cleared the ground floor for construction of the conference center, retaining a series of brick-vaulted spaces with large windows and masonry walls. The new center includes two conference rooms, a lecture hall, a dining room, a catering kitchen, and a flexible area adjacent to the dining room. We created a new loggia opposite the entrance for use as an informal gathering place, staff offices, bathrooms, and mechanical spaces.

The first floor, housing the family's tack, carriage, and automobile collections, was left intact as museum space open to the public. Renovation of the second floor required major intervention to completely transform the upper level staff quarters into guest rooms for conference guests. We transformed the hayloft into a common room and utilized the roof space to create an outdoor living room. To connect guests with the floors below, we widened the corridors and other public spaces, adding a new stairway. The curving walls and portals enhance the clarity of the circulation, leading guests back to the lower levels of the conference center.

5

0   16   32ft

6

Before

Before

5   Ground floor plan
6   Loggia looking into the conference room
7   Loggia

Before

8   First floor hallway
9   Lecture hall
10 New entry portal and vestibule
11 Loggia looking out towards new paved courtyard
12 Conference room

8

9

10

Before

11

Before

12

Before

13

14

13 Reconfigured hallway with new
    curving walls on the second floor
14 Second floor plan
15 Hayloft on the third floor
16 Kykuit
17 Fourth floor plan

15

16

Kykuit

Kykuit, the family house, required major infrastructure changes to meet modern life safety codes, to accommodate group tours of the first floor and art gallery, and to provide guest rooms on the upper floors. Our underlying preservation goal was to replace the heating, plumbing, life safety, and electrical systems without changing the original fabric of the 30,000-square-foot house. Moreover, all changes were designed to be reversible.

On the first and second floors we concealed all sprinkler heads in the pattern of the room moldings and rewired original light fixtures to provide ambient light and emergency lighting. We also installed a new heating system, sprinkler system, and fire doors. The third and fourth floors, originally staff quarters, were reconfigured and enlarged to become guest suites, continuing the scale, materials, and details of the original architecture.

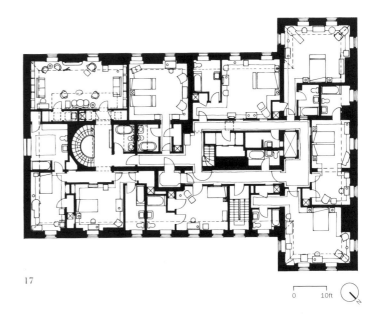

17

0   10ft

18

New furniture selections parallel the spirit of the original design, while the refurbished picture moldings and door and window trim sustain it. We chose new nickel-plated plumbing fixtures to simulate the old, and carefully fitted fire-rated doors, exit lights, emergency horns, and lighting into the existing architecture, ensuring that its historic character appears intact and undisturbed.

19

20

21

18   Dining room
19   Third floor guest suite
20&21   Guest suites
22   Music room

Duracell World Headquarters

Design/Completion 1993/1995
Bethel, Connecticut
The Duracell Corporation
310,000 square feet
Structural steel, red brick, glass floor tiles,
acoustical ceiling tiles, fabric wall coverings,
wood veneers, aluminum roofing shingles
(all from recycled or sustainable resources)

*As environmentally-minded corporate citizens,
the Duracell Corporation wanted its new world
headquarters to embody the ideals of
environmental sustainability and an
egalitarian corporate culture. Being familiar
with our work on school campuses, Duracell
believed that we would be able to design a
building that was consistent with their
collegial culture.*

Our response was to design a "corporate
campus" that blends naturally with the
rolling terrain of the Connecticut
woodlands, and incorporates recycled
products in 50 per cent of its construction.
The red brick gets its hue from scrap
manganese dioxide powder, a by-product
of Duracell's battery manufacturing
process. The structural steel is made
from recycled automobile bodies and
demolished buildings. The roofing
contains recycled aluminum, the floor tiles
contain recycled glass, and the acoustic
ceilings are made from recycled newsprint,
wood fibers and wool.

The three-story brick building has three
wings containing Duracell's corporate
offices, a data center, research and
laboratory facilities, a conference center
and TV/media center, exercise facilities,
and dining facilities. The wings maximize
perimeter office and work spaces with
views of the landscape while leaving an
unobtrusive footprint on the surrounding
land. They are linked on each floor by a
central circulation spine known as "Main
Street," which fosters communication
and community.

The design also includes a five-story garage
for 750 cars, which tucks into a hillside to
preserve the natural appearance of the
site, and a covered arcade to provide a
protected pedestrian link between the
garage and the headquarters building.

*When viewed from the exterior, the building is
episodic, revealing itself in small segments as
one drives or walks past it.*

1 Concept sketch
2 Entry detail
3 View through the woods
4 Entry
5 Site plan
6 Building plan

1

2

3

4

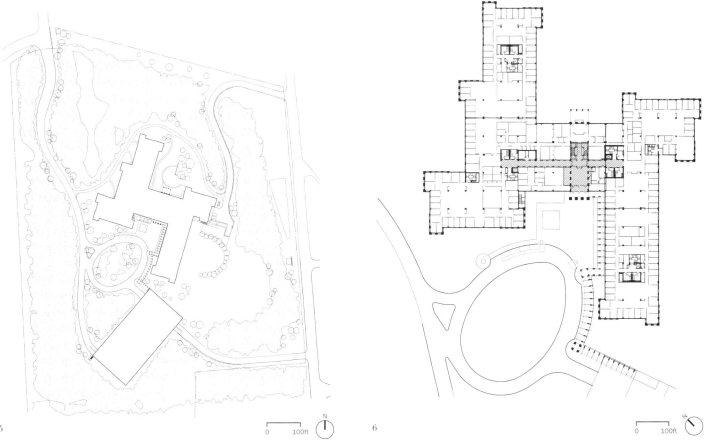

5

6

0   100ft   N

0   100ft   N

7

8

9

7 Second floor hallway
8 First floor hallway, Main Street
9 Ground floor hallway
Opposite:
   Entry stairwell detail

New Haven Union Station

Design/Completion 1980/1987
New Haven, Connecticut
City of New Haven; Federal Railway Agency
125,000 square feet
(300,000-square-foot attached parking garage)
Concrete-encased steel frame, brick, cast stone,
wood windows, oak trim, skylights, quarry tile walls,
stainless steel ceilings

*The essence of our design approach to Union
Station is the idea that everyone going to or
coming from a train will have to pass through
the main station space: the building becomes the
portal to the city.*

A Beaux Arts building designed in 1917
by Cass Gilbert, New Haven's Union
Station was a grand public building until
the decline of passenger railroads led to
its closing in 1954. Suffering from lack of
maintenance, extreme water damage, and
graffiti, it was almost demolished, but the
Northeast Corridor Improvement Project
came to the rescue in 1979.

We collaborated with Skidmore, Owings
& Merrill in the complete exterior and
interior restoration of Union Station, the
rebuilding of the dark tunnel passageways
leading to the train platforms, and the
construction of a connected commuter
parking garage. Moreover, nearly 70 years
after Gilbert designed Union Station, we
finally completed two components of his
original scheme: we built a canopy for the
main entrance and installed elevators and
escalators.

We completely cleaned and restored the
water-damaged ceilings, exterior masonry
and windows, the interior limestone walls,
and the chandeliers, clocks, ticket windows
and shop fronts. We installed new wooden
benches replicating the originals, and
removed offices on the balconies, allowing
natural light to flood through the arched
windows. New skylights and stainless steel
ceilings in the subways draw natural light
into once dark spaces.

The new parking garage has arches in its
facade, echoing the arches of Union
Station. They attempt to give the garage
a sense of lightness, reducing its scale in
relation to the historic railway building.

Before

1

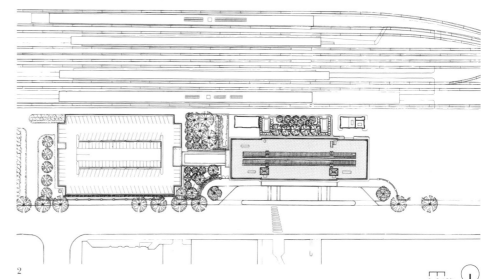
2

1   Garage and station
2   Site plan
3   Night view of entry

4

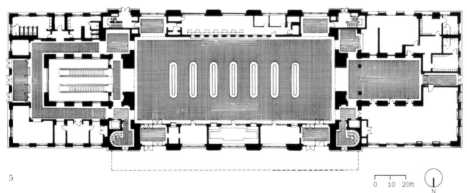

5

0 10 20ft

N

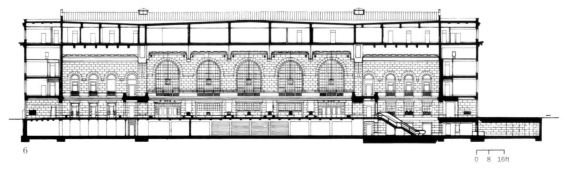

6

0 8 16ft

7

8

Before

4 Circulation to tracks
5 Floor plan
6 Section
7 Main waiting hall
8 Rendering of waiting hall

9

10

Before

9   Circulation tunnel to main waiting hall
10   Circulation tunnel to tracks
11   Garage façade
12   Basement floor plan

11

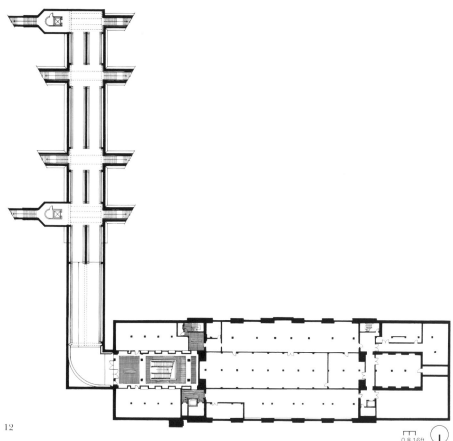

12

0 8 16ft N

New Haven City Hall

Design/Completion 1985/1993
New Haven, Connecticut
City of New Haven
115,000 square feet
Cast stone, brick, aluminum, white oak,
ceramic tile

Central to the new design of New Haven City Hall is the retention of the façade of the original building as the symbolic and functional main entrance to a new municipal complex. The new, six-story office annex extends the façade—an abstract version of the original City Hall—to the north, strengthening it in relation to the high-rise buildings on either side.

Designed by noted New Haven architect Henry Austin and completed in 1861, New Haven's City Hall is an exuberant early example of High Victorian Gothic architecture. Dominating the historic New Haven Green, it was listed on the National Register of Historic Places in 1975.

Combining preservation, restoration and new construction, its renewal is the culmination of a decades-long effort by citizens to preserve the building and incorporate it meaningfully into the new government center development.

The mayor's offices were returned to their original location overlooking the Green. The central four-story stair hall, which had been demolished, was reconstructed along with its original cast-iron staircase, skylight and vaulted ceiling.

One of the most important organizing elements in the restoration and addition to City Hall is the new colonnade, the largest public space in the building, which provides access to city agencies, the Aldermanic Chamber and the Hall of Records. The city agencies visited most often by the public are located on the colonnade's first floor. The Aldermanic Chamber, the heart of the municipal process, is located on the balcony level.

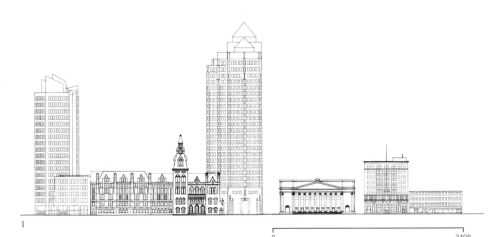

1

0   340ft

2

1 Elevation
2 Façade detail
3 Addition and restoration
Following pages:
   Entry facade

3

5

6

7

5   Entry stairwell
6   Colonnade
7   Detail of Aldermanic Chamber
8   Second floor plan
9   Ground floor plan
10   Aldermanic Chamber

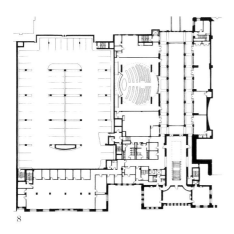

8

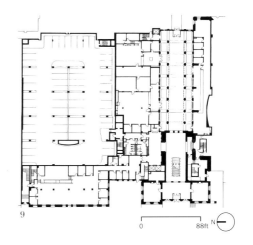

9

0   88ft   N

10

Yale University Art Gallery
Center for American Arts

Design/Completion 1974/1976
New Haven, Connecticut
Yale University
10,000 square feet
Cast-in-place concrete structure, fabric walls

The design explores the idea of "path" in a gathering place, and how a path might encourage people to move up close to a lecturer, resulting in a sense of intimacy and immediacy.

The existing art gallery consisted of a four-story 1920s Renaissance-style building with a 1950 addition designed by Louis Kahn. The only site available for new construction adjacent to the gallery was Weir Court, a secluded courtyard long considered beautiful for its shape, sense of enclosure and intimacy, and its proximity to the Kahn addition.

The program called for 8,000 square feet of new exhibition space, including administrative offices, and a 400-seat state-of-the-art lecture hall, which was to be linked to the art gallery but also have its own public entrance. The solution places the new auditorium under Weir Court, preserving three giant elms in the court that are integral to its success as an enclave of tranquil beauty.

The new auditorium is an intimate space for both large and small groups. It replaces an existing two-story lecture hall that was renovated into two floors of new gallery space. Gallery ceilings integrate the lighting within the structural grid, allowing for flexibility in the exhibit areas, as well as echoing the tetrahedral ceiling in the Kahn addition. The former sunken sculpture court on York Street was converted into gallery space through construction of a skylit roof, thus preserving the west facade of the Kahn building.

The auditorium is also reached through a network of existing stairs and passageways leading to Weir Court, which permit the new hall to be used when the gallery is closed.

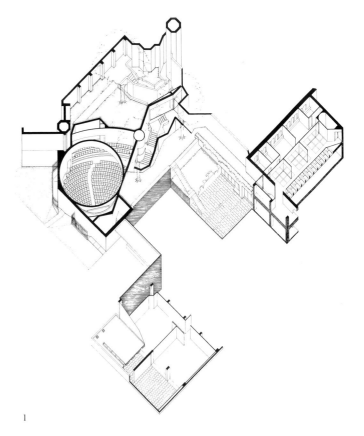

1

2

1   Axonometric
2   Sculpture garden
3   Lecture hall
4   Corridor to lecture hall
5   Gallery

138   Herbert S Newman and Partners

3

4

5

The Maritime Aquarium at Norwalk

Design/Completion 1995/1999
Norwalk, Connecticut
The Maritime Aquarium at Norwalk
150,000 square feet
Steel frame with masonry and glazed
curtain wall (new); structural timber
frame (existing)
Glass rotunda, glass conservatory exhibit
wings, glass marine tanks

*The Maritime Aquarium first opened
in the late 1980s as part of an urban
revitalization effort. After eight successful years
of operation, the aquarium had clarified its
mission and wanted to expand. Our master
plan gives the aquarium greater physical depth
by restructuring the entry, circulation and paths
and the linkage of its buildings, creating a more
dynamic setting for exploring and explaining
the aquatic world. The work will be completed in
two phases and is expected to increase visitor
attendance, enhance the overall ambience of the
streetscape and provide additional parking.*

In the first phase, now under construction,
an adjacent old industrial building will
become the aquarium's Environmental
Education Center, housing state-of-the-art
demonstration laboratories, lecture
rooms, a gift shop and a restaurant. It will
be linked to the main building by a
concourse leading to a spiral glass
rotunda, the new iconic image of the
aquarium and its main entrance, which
will bring visual and experiential
excitement to the precinct. Visitors will
make the transition from the everyday into
the realm of the sea, winding around a

circular water exhibit from the street
to the lobby and main exhibit level.

The second phase will consist of a series
of enhancements to the interior of the
main building, which will be laid out in
thematic neighborhoods like a town.
A central circulation axis will act as a
street, organizing the spaces. Exhibit
rooms will branch out into wings
containing coastal and deep water exhibits
and discovery labs. A central reception/
exhibit space, Falconer Hall, will be an
interior "square" crossed by the street
linking to views of the river.

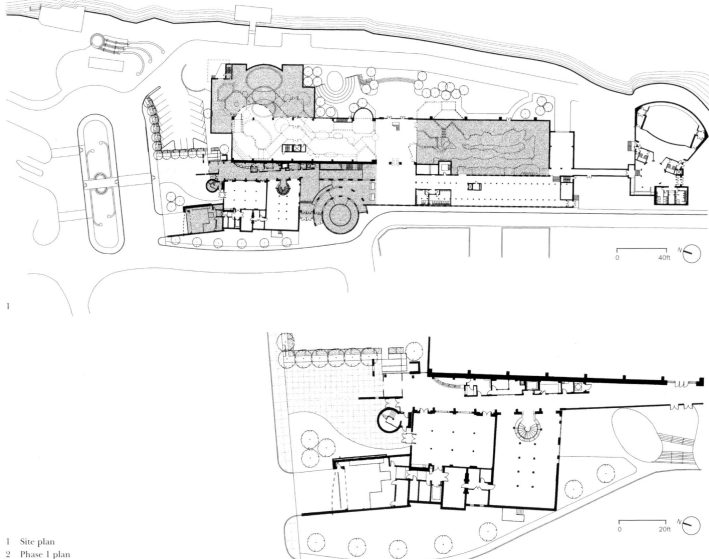

1

2

1 Site plan
2 Phase 1 plan
3 Computer rendering of Phase 1 entry

3

Westport Public Library

Design/Completion 1995/1998
Westport, Connecticut
Westport Public Library
16,000 square feet (new)
Steel frame with masonry veneer
curtain wall construction

*Our addition and renovation of this 1984
Gwathmey Siegel design moves away from the
abstraction of open plan and the idea of
building as sculpture, to a notion of identifiable
rooms and a village of forms. Neither approach
is better than the other; it is a matter of
responding to present programmatic
requirements that require discrete spaces
for the complex needs of today's library.*

A town library is an emblem of civic pride.
The Westport Library has long been an
important town resource and meeting
place, but its structure was lacking
appropriate circulation and space to meet
enhanced use, and required expansion.
Our solution was to renovate the original
library, and design a new addition that
meets the needs of its growing community
and new technology.

The 16,000-square-foot addition provides
book stack expansion and reading rooms
that overlook the Saugatuck River and
Jessup Green. The children's department
and the audio/visual department were
expanded. The new spaces improve the
library's ability to conduct its many day
and evening programs, and allow it to add
future services including office space for
business people, a video library, and a
coffee bar.

The library entrance has been moved in
order to be accessible from a reconfigured
town green. Reception areas, circulation
and reference departments were
reconfigured and expanded. A new
circulation desk and reception area were
added.

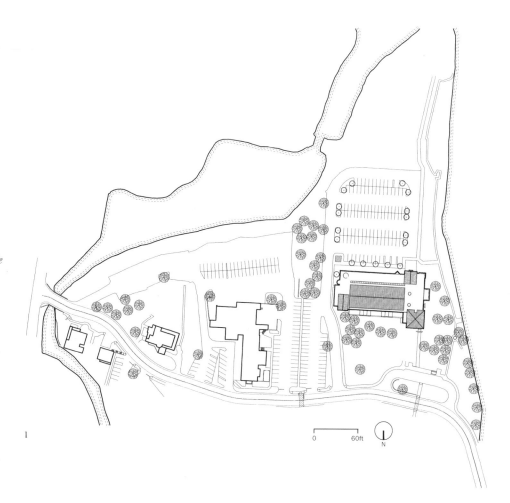

1

0   60ft   N

2

3

Before

4

1   Site plan
2   View of entry from across the river
3   View of river courtyard
4   River elevation

5

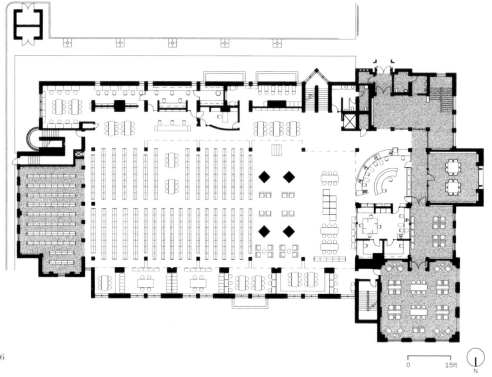

6

0   15ft

N

7

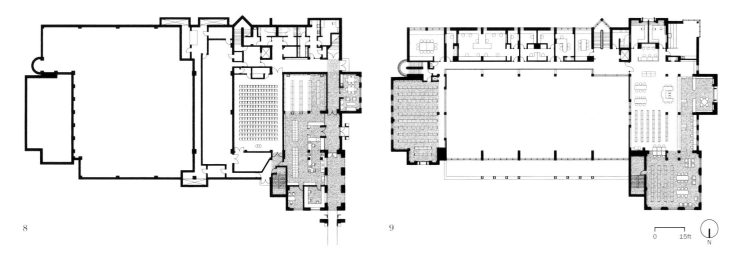

8   9

Bridgeport Federal Courthouse Annex

Design/Completion 1988/1992
Bridgeport, Connecticut
United States General Services Administration
15,000 square feet
Steel frame, synthetic stucco, painted steel roof, aluminum-frame windows, carpets and limestone flooring, oak veneer paneling

Our addition to the 1960s Bridgeport Federal Courthouse building recalls a nearly lost prototype from antiquity—the civic temple—which remains the pride of many American cities, whether in the form of a courthouse, a town hall, a library or a post office. We wanted to pay homage to the roots of our Western system of justice, honoring its classical beginnings and spirit.

An important model for this design was Faneuil Hall in Boston, Massachusetts, where the life of the street extends inside on the first floor and civic activities take place on the level above. In the Courthouse Annex, justice functions are elevated for reasons of dignity and security. An economical rectangular volume encloses two courtrooms, two sets of judges' chambers, plus conference rooms, offices, and ancillary spaces. The lower level, following classical models, is a podium for practical use, in this case, parking.

The temple form gives the annex prominence amid elevated expressways and a big downtown shopping mall, and the tired, monochromatic urban setting is enlivened by the colorful window frames and applied decoration—ideas again informed by ancient models. The exterior ornament was designed by Kent Bloomer.

1 Site plan
2 Façade detail
3 Façade rendering
4 Corner view
5 Level two floor plan

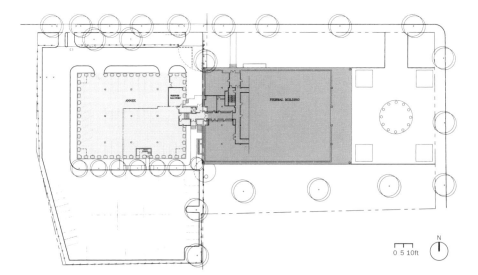

1

2

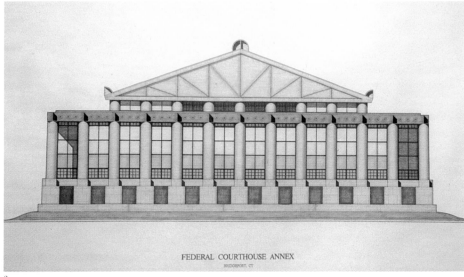

FEDERAL COURTHOUSE ANNEX
BRIDGEPORT, CT

3

4

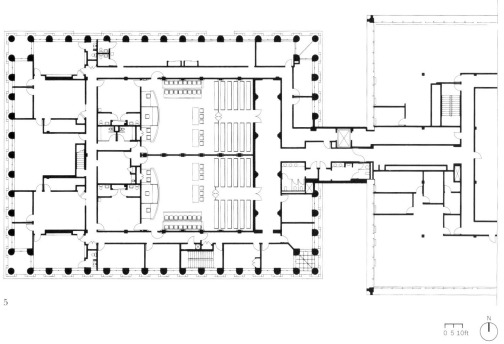

5

Richard's of Greenwich

Design/Completion 1996/2000
Greenwich, Connecticut
The Mitchell Family
35,000 square feet/338 parking spaces
Steel frame superstructure, reinforced concrete
Brick, stone, aluminum wall panels, cast stone,
single-ply membrane roof, ornamental aluminum

Downtown districts in towns can succeed as an urbane response to suburban shopping malls. Our design attempts to create a "House of Richards" with a dignity that is missing from contemporary urban retail architecture. Without pandering to the past on heterogeneous Greenwich Avenue, the design attempts to demonstrate a love of craft and grace reflective of the store's philosophy and the clothing it sells.

The new two-story, 35,000-square-foot clothing store replaces the original Richard's, a 9,000-square-foot shop once located directly across the street. The design attempts to contribute to the streetscape of the avenue, and ameliorate the downtown's chronic parking and traffic problems by providing off-street parking at street level and in an underground parking garage.

Street level adjacent parking is a convenience that allows an urban merchant to compete with suburban shopping center attractions. In this case, the store is a metaphor for the house on a main urban street with its fenced "backyard garden," including a parking area on a side street.

1

2

3

1–3   Model
   4   Rendering of Greenwich Avenue façade

150   Herbert S Newman and Partners

4

MICA Corporate Headquarters

Design/Completion 1996/1999
Shelton, Connecticut
MICA Corporation
25,000 square feet
Structural steel frame, brick block,
precast sills, aluminum sunscreen
and window overhangs, limestone floor

The MICA Corporation, an international producer of adhesives for food packaging, required a new expanded headquarters building to house their main manufacturing and warehousing facilities together with administrative, sales, and laboratory uses. Having acquired a large wooded and hilly site with views to the Housatonic River valley, the company wanted a design that capitalized on the site's natural attributes in a manner consistent with its goals of simplicity in design and long-term value in building quality.

The plan organizes the building into two principle wings: a two-story office and laboratory wing and a double-height manufacturing and warehousing wing. They are arranged on the site to make a main entry court for visitors and office workers, and a manufacturing service court for material handling and product loading. A large precinct of woodland and rock outcrops has been preserved and is reached by a footbridge from the second floor dining space.

The building is massed to reinforce the access drive, which, in the form of a spiral, ascends from the public street onto the plateau of the developed site, culminating in an entry hall and conference room as the entry sequence destination. The large conference room sits high on the site, commanding views down the river valley. A mix of brick masonry and concrete masonry units articulate the assembly and hierarchy of the building components.

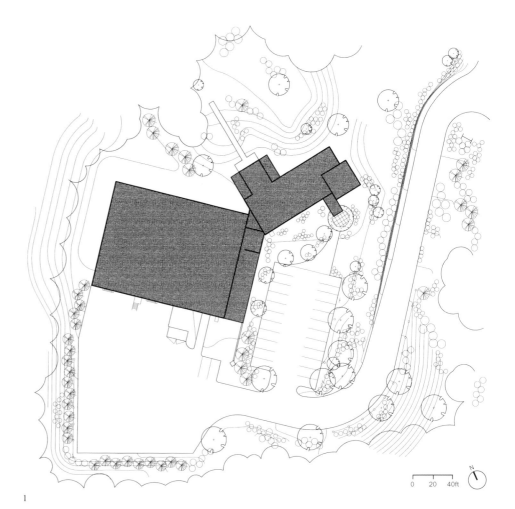

1

2

1   Site plan
2   Side elevation
3   View from the east
4   Second floor plan

3

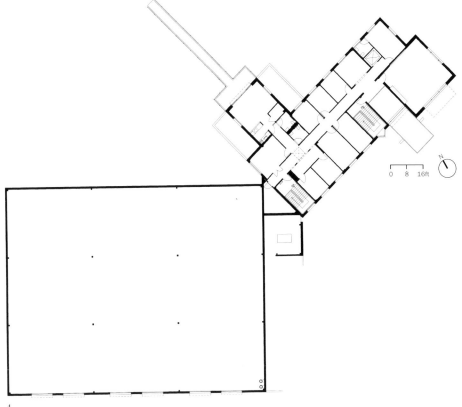

4

Chapel Square Mall

Design/Completion 1983/1985
New Haven, Connecticut
The Rouse Company
540,000 square feet (new);
75,000 square feet (renovated)
Steel trusses, quarry tile floors, ceramic tile
partitions, plexiglass skylights, fabric banners

When it was built in the early 1960s, Chapel Square Mall was one of the first urban malls in the country, but by 1980 it was suffering from a tired, tarnished image. Our redesign, modeled after the great nineteenth century galleries of Italy and America, attempts to make the mall a more inviting urban space.

Skylights brighten the once dreary spaces with natural light, allowing trees to grow inside the mall. Painted steel arches and a sky blue ceiling ringed with translucent banners that can be changed seasonally complete the transition to a European-style galleria shopping street.

Natural materials—quarry tile floors, oak handrails and benches, a water fountain, and trees and plants in terracotta pots—help reinforce the illusion that this space is an exterior one. A performance stage used for promotional purposes, pushcarts selling local arts and crafts, and "Tivoli" lights lend festive marketplace atmosphere to the mall.

On the second floor, a new food court is connected to the existing mall by a common outdoor cafe-style dining area. The entrance is announced by an "apse" at the end of the galleria. Behind the apse, cafe-style shops lead to the east and west, and finally to the north, which has been opened up with glazing to re-establish Chapel Square Mall's connection to the New Haven Green.

While we used the great nineteenth century galleries as models for our redesign, the basic problem remains: an urban interior mall, unlike the galleria model, takes people off the streets and diminishes the life of the city.

1

1 Galleria
2 Section
3 View of upper level

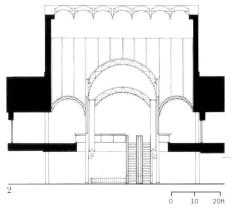

2

0   10   20ft

Before

3

Gant Shirt Factory

Design 1967
New Haven, Connecticut
Gant Shirtmakers
250,000 square feet

Our design for the Gant Shirt Factory was an attempt at creating an architecture for the open road that would stand up to the scale of the vast new highways of the period. This is a problem that had never been explored before.

The site was an industrial corridor facing the Connecticut Turnpike, a busy highway leading up the New England coast. Because passing motorists would see it from the road, Gant wanted to convey a progressive, dynamic impression of its new manufacturing plant.

The design responds by utilizing large-scale details, earth forms, a reflecting pool, and abstract geometric forms to create a strong, easily perceived image for motorists driving by at 60 miles per hour. In the same manner, the interiors are amenable and visually stimulating to employees.

On the second floor, a wide clerestory-lit interior street links administrative departments. A pitched roof hides many small roof protuberances, while the reflecting pool, plaza and circular garden outside the cafeteria create visual relief.

1

1   Concept sketch
2&3   Model

2

3

Guilford Community Center

Design/Completion 1989/1993
Guilford, Connecticut
Town of Guilford
24,000 square feet
Steel frame, brick veneer
Carpet, quarry and ceramic tile, hardwood floors,
painted drywall with wainscotting

The idea of a main street that serves to bring the community together informed the design of Guilford Community Center, which features a spine of circulation and path that orders its various rooms. The scale and texture are compatible with the town's well-preserved New England fabric of clapboard houses, churches and stores. The center is located within the Guilford Historic District.

The building accommodates the diverse programmatic needs of many constituencies from the Guilford community. These needs include a daytime senior center, a preschool, after-school programs for gymnastics and aerobics, meeting rooms for clubs and town agencies, headquarters for the Parks and Recreation Department, an arts and ceramics studio, and the broadcast control center and studio for the Guilford community cable television channel.

The center includes a large activity room with a kitchen. It is used for dances, receptions, and other events, as well as daily senior dining and a meals-on-wheels program. Accessibility for the handicapped and life safety considerations are important for the senior citizen and preschool users of the community center. All spaces for these groups are clustered on the first floor.

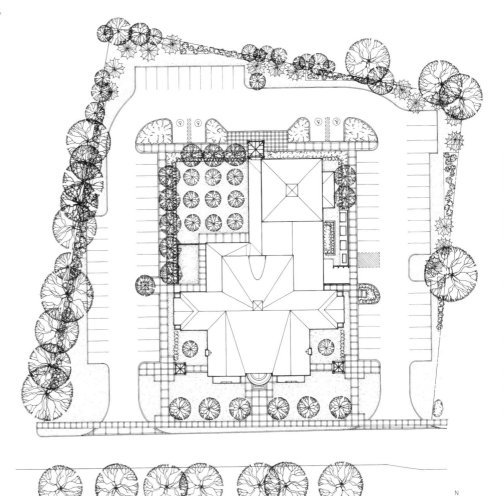

1

0 10 20ft N

2

1 Site plan
2 Rear view
3 Entry elevation
4 First floor plan

3

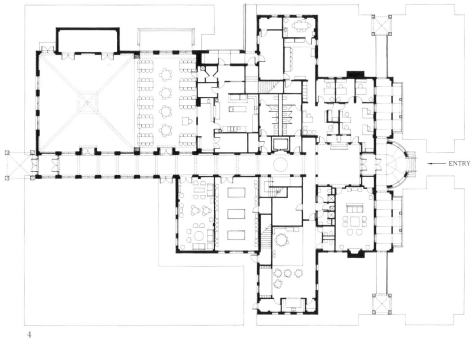

4

ENTRY

0 5 10ft

N

5

5   Community room exterior
Opposite:
    Community room interior

Yale University
Central Power Plant

Design/Completion 1994/1999
New Haven, Connecticut
45,000 square feet
Steel, concrete, concrete block, brick

The expansion and modernization of this historic power plant required great sensitivity to the site, the landscape, surrounding views, and acoustical issues. Our addition attempts to retain the pre-eminence of the powerful yet human-scaled expansion of the original 1929 building. By continuing the massing, materials and scale amid surrounding buildings, it reinforces the edge of a new major outdoor space for the campus.

Bounded by the Yale Hall of Graduate Studies, the Payne Whitney Gymnasium, Stiles and Morse Colleges, and the new Residence Hall, the power plant is adjacent to the historic Grove Street Cemetery and Tower Parkway, a major vehicular artery.

Part of a larger effort to modernize and connect Yale's three power plants, this renovated plant will provide 13.5 megawatts of electricity as primary and emergency power sources for the Yale campus. In addition, the facility has been designed to be the primary source for campus steam and chilled water, and a reliable source of electricity to the university, improving fuel efficiency, reducing air emissions, and lowering Yale's operating costs.

We worked in collaboration with the Kuljian Corporation, an engineering firm in Philadelphia, and the Yale community to find solutions to the complex visual, functional, and engineering problems involved in the expansion. We attempted a seamlessness between the old and new power plant and an integration with the neighborhood.

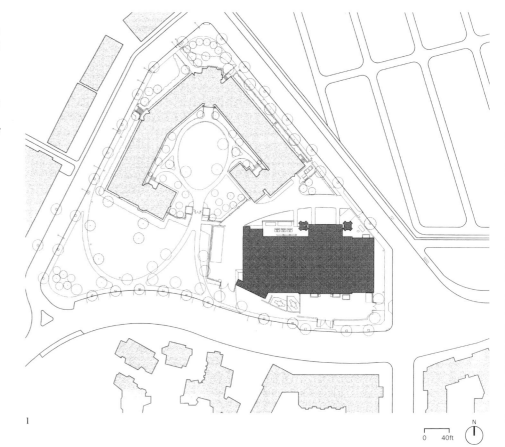

1

0   40ft   N

1   Site plan
2   View of Payne Whitney
     Gymnasium between Power Plant
     and New Residence Hall
3   Gate detail
4   Floor plan

Before

2

3

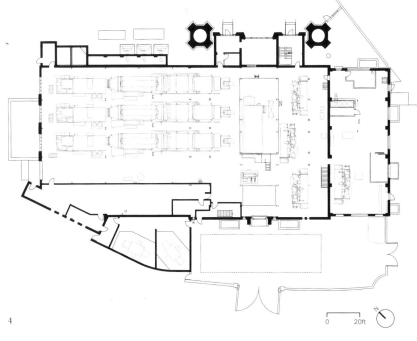

4

0   20ft

5

6

7

5 View of addition from Tower Parkway
6 Rendering of Power Plant and New Residence Hall
7 View from York Square Place
8 Section
9 View from Ashmun Street

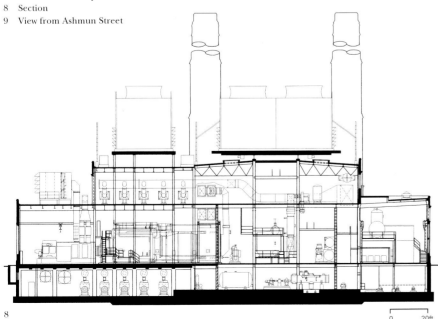

8

0   20ft

9

Athletic/Recreational

Wesleyan University
Freeman Athletic Center

Design/Completion 1987/1990
Middletown, Connecticut
Wesleyan University
100,000 square feet (new);
10,000 square feet (renovated)
Supported concrete slab foundation,
steel-frame roofs, brick, cast stone,
ceramic tile

*Our approach to the Freeman Athletic Center,
which is programmed for intramural, not intercollegiate use, is based on the idea of making a
place from which one can choose to observe or
participate in a range of athletic pursuits.*

Our design brings together activities
previously scattered across the Wesleyan
University campus by incorporating an
existing hockey rink into a new complex
sited at the heart of the university's
playing fields, and creating a new eight-
lane 400-meter track and soccer field.

The athletic center is a cluster of buildings,
each with its own identity. The new field
house, natatorium, administrative center,
and existing hockey rink are linked by a
main lobby designed to encourage
participation in the activities of the center.
It gives spectators access to the existing
grandstand seating in the hockey rink,
the new grandstand in the natatorium,
and the field house. Administrative offices
are located off the lobby.

The field house has an open flexible
space for recreational, intramural
and intercollegiate athletics, including
a 200-meter track, tennis, basketball and
volleyball courts, an indoor track and
field area, and practice surfaces for all
field sports. The natatorium includes a
50-meter by 25-yard pool and fixed seating
for 300 spectators. The pool's length
accommodates a shallow instructional
area, a competition area and a deep end
for diving. The center also has a multi-use
room for exercise, wrestling, aerobics, and
martial arts. Other facilities include weight
training rooms, locker rooms, offices, and
classrooms.

1   Entry court

2

3

4

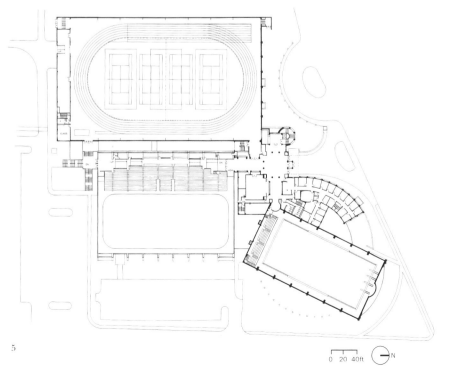

5

6

2   Entry hall
3   Field house
4   Natatorium
5   First floor plan
6   Natatorium exterior

0   20   40ft

Yale University
Cullman Indoor Tennis Courts

Design/Completion 1972/1973
New Haven, Connecticut
Yale University
30,000 square feet
Brick and steel

This design examines the issue of how to foster the participation and engagement of people in the sport of tennis through architecture.

Completed in 1973, Cullman Indoor Tennis Courts have been the prototype for a number of indoor courts built in the United States. They were among the first to use indirect lighting in a prefabricated building, and the first to place bleachers above support services for viewing intercollegiate and tournament games.

The project is really two structures: one inside the other. The outer structure is an inexpensive metal shell with a polyurethane playing surface. The inner structure is a low, linear volume housing a free-standing locker room and lounge. From inside the smaller structure, viewers can watch games in progress on either side. The courts are paired and spaced apart, minimizing interferences that may distract players' concentration.

The metal industrial building has a brick façade to unite it visually with surrounding buildings on the athletic fields.

1

1 View of lounge and grandstand from the courts
2 Lounge and viewing area
3 Floor plan

2

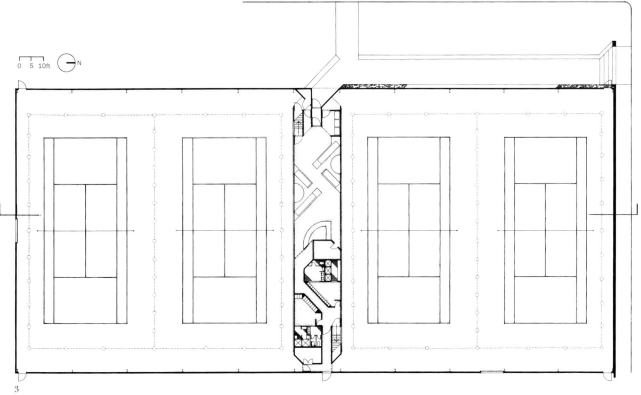

3

Milford Jai Alai

Design/Completion 1974/1977
Milford, Connecticut
Milford Jai Alai
150,000 square feet
Steel frame, long-span steel trusses, reinforced concrete walls, exposed block
Painted gypsum board, oak veneer interiors

The design concept attempts to create an urbane, festive environment that is colorful and fun. The "galleria" space is the key both to the functioning of the circulation within the whole facility and to the sense of festivity.

There are two main entrances: one for valet parking and one for self-parking; both are connected by the galleria. From the main entrance the galleria steps up two levels corresponding to the slope of the site and the spectator grandstand. Moving through the space under colorful banners, visitors can enter a 250-seat restaurant and bar to their right, or a betting lounge to the left. Escalators lead up to a second level which contains a small bar and a second betting room.

A second flight of escalators leads to a third level. Off its lobby is another entrance; to the right is the 10,000-square-foot International Room, which displays the games on a 12 by 15-foot rear projection screen; to the left is a third betting lounge.

The 4,800-seat grandstand is an unobstructed space 180 feet wide and spanned by exposed steel trusses 30 feet on center. These trusses cantilever 60 feet beyond to form the galleria and restaurant, and extend beyond as a sunshade. The focus of everything is the playing court—180 feet long, 50 feet wide, 48 feet high, bright green, and lit to a level of 176 footcandles at the center court.

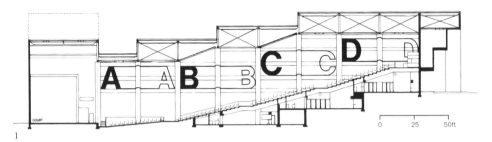

1

2

3

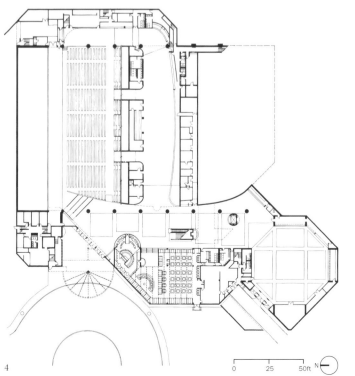

1 Section
2 International room
3 Interior view
4 Ground floor plan
5 Building façade
6 Interior view
7 Entry detail
Following pages:
 Entry façade

4

5

6

7

Teletrack Theater

Design/Completion 1976/1979
New Haven, Connecticut
General Instrument Corporation
70,000 square feet
Structural steel

At Teletrack Theater, the first off-track betting theater in the world, up to 2,300 people can watch live horse races on a large television screen and bet as they would at the race track. The design of the theater responds to the particular needs of contemporary society, while seeking an ambience of wonder, excitement, glitter and escape, much like the movie palaces of the 1930s.

The site is a 10-acre flat parcel at the junction of two major interstate highways at New Haven Harbor. The building form relates in scale to the harbor and oil tanks, and to the intersecting ribbon of highways, while advertising the theater's presence.

We wanted to provide an environment that would enhance the experience of watching a television image of a live sporting event. Because horse races are traditionally short, we also needed to create an atmosphere of excitement and festivity for the times between races. The program called for betting windows, private and public dining rooms, fast food concessions, bars and other typical race track amenities. The overhanging boxes of the Clubhouse Lounge and the tiered levels of the public dining rooms wrap around the theater, making it possible for all patrons to see the 24-foot by 32-foot screen clearly and comfortably.

A mural of racing horses dominates the lobby; neon sculpture heightens the sense of excitement and anticipation as patrons move toward the theater. The curved stair and access ramp of the concourse provide clear, direct circulation routes into the theater, while diminishing amounts of ambient light enable daytime patrons to become gradually accustomed to the dark interior.

1

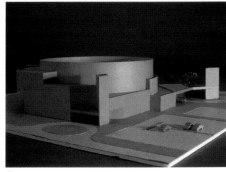

2

1&2 Model
3 Entry elevation
4 Entry detail
5 Interior rendering

3

4

5

6

7

8

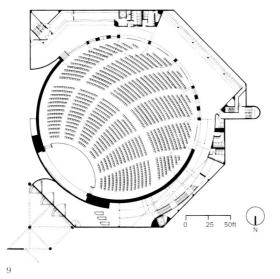

9

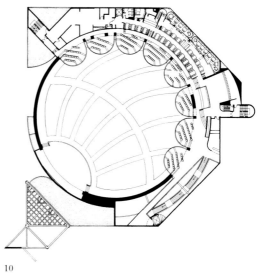

10

6   Balcony
7   Interior rendering
8   Side elevation
9   Second level plan
10 Third level plan

Yale University Athletic Fields

New Haven, Connecticut
Yale University

Our studies of Yale University's existing athletic complex in the mid-1980s provided recommendations for the renovation, expansion, upgrading, and modification of some of its aging facilities, and the addition of new facilities to meet the university's pressing space needs. Our work included creating a new campus for these activities with a major spine and cross-axis of pedestrian circulation. Subsequently, Edward Larrabee Barnes designed a new tennis center at one axis, and we have completed a number of projects along the spine.

Coxe Cage Field House
A fully renovated 1925 field house, with a new 200-meter tuned track, seating for 1,200, training and support facilities, and a new weight room.

Soccer/Lacrosse Stadium
A varsity playing field transformed from a large lawn area into a public stadium for intercollegiate soccer and lacrosse.

Golf Course Clubhouse
A remodeled and expanded clubhouse, with a new pro shop, conference facility, and a 100-seat "grill room."

Dewitt Cuyler Sports Complex
A renovated 21-acre complex, with a modernized university track, two football practice fields, a JV baseball diamond, and a freshman football field located inside the track.

Yale Bowl Press Box
A new press box to replace the original that was destroyed by fire.

Cullman Indoor Tennis Courts
A new four-court indoor tennis facility with bleachers and viewing area.

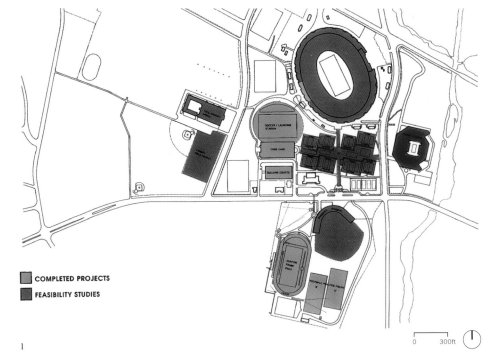

■ COMPLETED PROJECTS
■ FEASIBILITY STUDIES

1

0   300ft

1   Site plan
2   Aerial view of site

2

Yale University
Coxe Cage Field House

Design/Completion 1980/1981
New Haven, Connecticut
Yale University
4-lane, 200-meter indoor track
Steel frame and masonry, glass skylights

When renovating Coxe Cage in 1980, our intent was to transform the 1925 field house into a modern athletic facility for indoor track and field competitions and general field house needs while preserving its historic integrity.

We designed a new lighting system to complement the repaired roof and installed a new, resilient 200-meter tuned track with multi-use flooring suitable for basketball, baseball, and lacrosse practice. The grandstand was situated along the track with seating for 1,200 spectators. All interior finishes were restored.

New weight training rooms, batting cages, and support facilities were added below the grandstands.

1

2

1 Interior
2 Grandstand detail
3 Interior view

3

Religious

Williams College Jewish Religious Center

Design/Completion 1988/1991
Williamstown, Massachusetts
Williams College
5,000 square feet
Wood frame with cedar siding, metal and rubber
membrane roofing, oak floors, aluminum windows

Jewish religious buildings have typically
been adaptations of traditional regional
types. Following this pattern, the Williams
College Jewish Religious Center is a
wooden building painted white and given
monumental scale by a dominant vertical
element. Following the vernacular, the
interior is also painted white.

However, more particular concepts inform
this synagogue's design. "Synagogue," for
example, is derived from the Greek word
for meeting. So, while this building has
many functions that are conducted
separately, its interior has the character
of a single space and can be opened up
to form one large room.

Similarly, since reading has been integral
to worship throughout the history of
Jewish religious observance, the presence
of light is fundamental. Therefore, the
white, naturally lit interior assumes a
significance particular to the Jewish
religious experience, and the tall form
rises from the center of the sanctuary as
the source of light.

Central to virtually all religious experience
is the mountain. The dominant form of
this building remembers Mount Moriah
and Mount Sinai, while evoking the recent
memory of the Holocaust by allusion to
the form of the chimney.

Because High Holy Day services and events
such as weddings and bar mitzvahs may
require seating up to 300, while typical
Friday evening services are for about 50,
the sanctuary is expandable. The intimacy
and ritual participation by congregants,
an essential part of Jewish liturgy, is
maintained through both configurations.

1   Section
2   Entry elevation
3   Side elevation
Opposite:
    Building in context

5

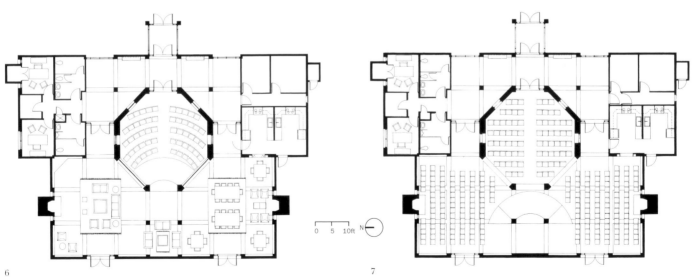

6   7

8

9

10

Yale University
Battell Chapel

Completion 1983
New Haven, Connecticut
Yale University
17,000 square feet
Paint, gold leaf, carpeting, red oak woodwork

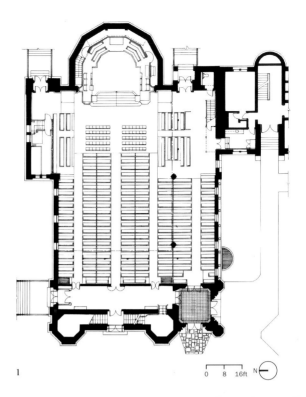

The architect Russell Sturgis built Battell Chapel for Yale University in 1876. It was much admired then for its gilding, bright stenciling, mosaic tile art, and painted and oiled woodwork. In the 1920s, however, the Victorian interior was painted over to emulate stone, as Yale turned to a collegiate Gothic style.

When the university hired us to renovate Battell's interior, our initial research yielded clues to the original design hidden beneath the faux stone, convincing us that Battell needed to be restored. Yale agreed.

We replicated the original stenciling in gold leaf and fifteen painted colors, refurbished the wood paneling and pews, re-upholstered seat cushions, installed new carpeting, and replaced the brass railings in the balconies.

We modified the apse, the focal point of the chapel, to accommodate a small orchestra or small religious service. Retaining the character of the original lighting, we designed new wall sconces reminiscent of the original gas jets, and cleaned and rewired the chandeliers to a sophisticated control board which adjusts the lighting intensity in the space.

We converted the outmoded gravity heating system to forced air heating, concealed vents and sprinklers, and excavated the basement to create restrooms and to provide better access to mechanical equipment. We added ramps to allow access for the disabled, replaced the roof with new slates which replicate the original fish-scale pattern, and repointed the entire sandstone facade.

1 Floor plan
2 View from apse
3 Balcony view of organ
Following pages:
   View of apse

Before

3

B'nai Israel Synagogue

Design/Completion 1998/2000
Southbury, Connecticut
Congregation B'nai Israel
22,000 square feet
Wood frame, white stained siding, shingle roof,
painted gypsum board, oak paneling

Because this site occupies the rural
pastureland of a historic district, we chose
barn-like forms strung out on a hillside
along the edge of a woodland. Large forms
work in rural historic districts when they
evoke historic precedents. The synagogue,
which is 800 feet from the road, reveals
itself in detail as one approaches it.

The program called for the traditional
triumvirate of uses: sanctuary, social hall,
and school. As in the Williams College
Jewish Religious Center, the plan provides
for expansion of the sanctuary for the
High Holy Days, and does not compromise
the intimacy and engagement of the
congregants in the service when it grows
from 150 to 500 people.

The forms are broken into a string of
buildings to break the scale and identity
of the parts. The plan is bent to form
a necklace on the contours, creating
a private campus space around an
existing pond in the rear.

1 Site plan
2 Sanctuary
3 Sanctuary detail
4 Entry elevation rendering
5 Building plan

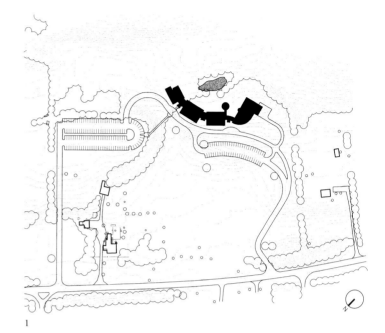

1

2

3

4

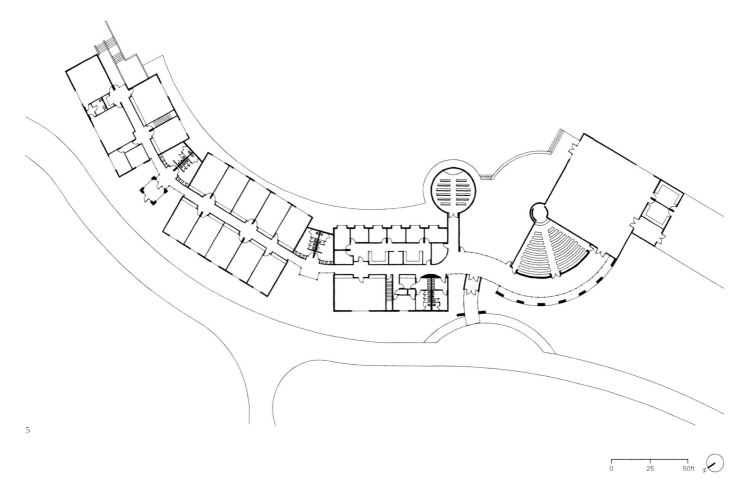

5

0   25   50ft

Residential

Winnick Residence

Design/Completion 1962/1963
Woodbridge, Connecticut
The Winnick Family
4,000 square feet
Wood frame on concrete block foundation,
white stucco finish, quarry, vinyl and
ceramic tile floor

By creating a variety of spatial experiences
in this house—the dining room is only
seven feet high, while the living room
extends to the full eighteen-foot height
of the house—a wide range of freedom is
given the family within an ordered
discipline, establishing gathering and
private spaces. The system of projecting
wings zones different activities within a
compact plan.

The first architectural commission for
the architect upon graduation from
architectural school, the house pays
homage to the ideas of Mies and Kahn
in its attempt to create hierarchy of use,
geometry of structure and plan, use of
natural light, and attention to details.

The house's four U-shaped wings are
arranged in pinwheel fashion to create
discrete views and outdoor zones. They
open to a garden and terrace off the living
room and dining room, a sunken garden
off the west wing, and balconies off the
bedrooms. They provide the living spaces,
while the interstices include kitchen,
bathroom, laundry and circulation space,
which widens into a gallery on the lower
level and a family sitting room on the
upper level.

The house rests on a sloping site. Its levels
are connected by a staircase built around
a skylit open space. The roof is raised on
support posts to create surrounding bands
of clerestory windows.

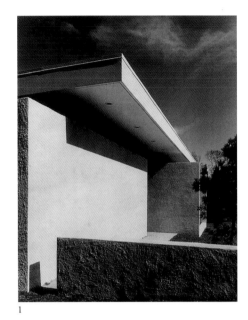

1

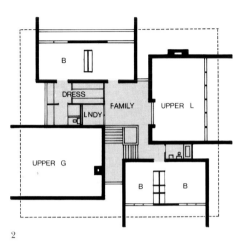

2

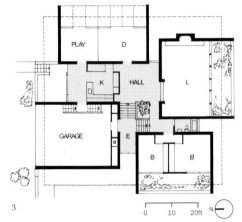

3

1   Entrance
2   First floor plan
3   Ground floor plan
4   Living room elevation

4

Kramer Residence

Design/Completion 1981/1984
Stamford, Connecticut
The Kramer Family
8,000 square feet
Cedar planking, red oak, cherry wood
and local stone

The owners admire the work of Frank
Lloyd Wright, so we attempted to make
a house in which Frank Lloyd Wright
leaves the prairie and settles in New
England. The plan and ordering
principles of the house are informed
by the ideas of Wright and Louis Kahn.

Combining Wrightean themes with
traditional New England architecture,
this long, rambling wood house clings
to the Mianus riverbank only 25 feet away.
Facing the water along a north–south
route, it repeats horizontal lines, broad
shaded overhangs and a heavy, natural
stone foundation. The east elevation
faces distant houses, offering New England
village neighborliness while maintaining
privacy and order.

Entering from a walkway under the trees
east of the house, one is guided directly
onto the east–west path facing a small
window seat belvedere, with a splendid
river view. The principal path runs parallel
to the river and is washed by natural light
from multi-shaped windows and gabled
skylights. Spaces of differing size and
height unfold to the north and south.

The master bedroom, dining and living
rooms, two studies, and primary outer
terrace all are octagonal forms. The
building materials are natural, with
similar colors inside and out. Exterior
cedar planking is complemented by red
oak in the interior. Fireplaces and other
elements are built of stone from the
property.

1

2

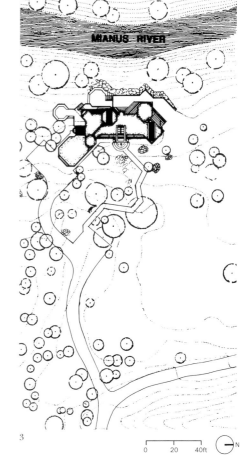

1   Front elevation
2   Model
3   Site plan
Opposite:
    River view, rear elevation

3

0   20   40ft

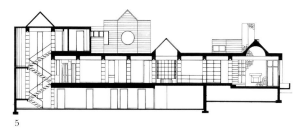

5

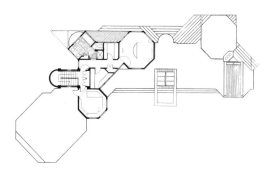

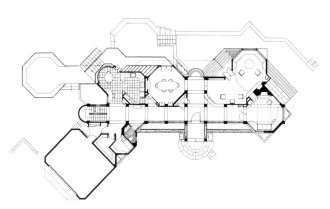

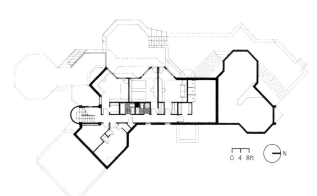

6

7

8

0 4 8ft   N

5   Sections
6   Floor plans
7   Dining room
8   Side elevation
9   Gallery

Round Hill Residence

Design/Completion 1982/1991
Woodbridge, Connecticut
Herbert S. Newman
4,300 square feet
Central octagonal element of bearing
brick masonry, steel tube framed and
braced tower

Set near the top of a hillside overlooking
Long Island Sound, the house looks to
Palladian antecedents of symmetry and
place: the design concept is a tower
supported by a large center hall. Skylights
surround the tower, separating it from the
rest of the house and bringing light into
the center hall.

The structural order creates voids in the
system that allow light to enter and
energize the interior spaces, evoking a
hierarchical ordering of structure and
space. The central hall becomes the
confluence of paths, light, and space.
The living room is treated as a bay window
expanding on the central axis outside the
brick octagon to the south, and other
spaces grow laterally from the octagon.

The siting of the 500-square-foot library
completes the entry courtyard. The notion
of transparency led to the idea of its
temple form, reminiscent of Greek Revival
architecture. The portico continues the
theme of colonnades found in the house,
and the glass pediment reinforces the
transparency.

1

1   Front entrance and library
2   Southeast elevation
3   Night view with pool and living room
4   First floor plan

2

3

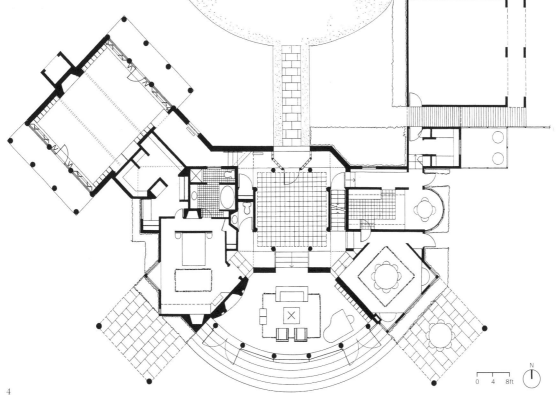

4

0   4   8ft   N

5

5 Observatory
6 Living room
Opposite:
    Entry hall

6

9

Previous pages:
    Rear elevation
9   Library elevation
10   Library
Opposite:
    Entry hall with view of
    living room and
    dining room

10

12   Section
13   Living room with view to entry hall
Opposite:
    Stair to third floor

OBSERVATORY

BEDROOM   BATH   BATH   BEDROOM

DRESSING   BATH   ENTRY
HALL   KITCHEN   BREAKFAST

12

0   4   8ft

13

Planning and Design

The Arts Center District
– Whitney/Grove

Design/Completion 1979/1988
New Haven, Connecticut
H. Pierce Company
140,000 square feet office and retail space;
37 townhouses
Brick, cast stone, copper, slate,
cherry paneling

*New Haven's Arts Center District is an
important gateway to downtown New Haven
and the campus of Yale University. In an effort
to revitalize the precinct in the 1980s, we
collaborated with city agencies, non-profit
groups, and private developers to produce a
master plan that mixes offices, shops, galleries,
restaurants, low-rise housing and parking
garages. At both Audubon Court and Whitney/
Grove, a raised courtyard with parking below
creates a new, secure outdoor living room for
residents, while providing communal activity
along the city streets.*

Streets are the most important spaces in
cities. When special attention is given to
the layering of scales and placing of like
uses on both sides, a healthy street is the
result. These ideas influenced our design
of Whitney/Grove.

Although its uses are diverse, Whitney/
Grove is carefully integrated into the
neighborhood by its curbs, sidewalks,
street furniture, fences and hedges, stoops,
and portals. At one end of the site, facing
toward New Haven's office precinct, it is
an eight-story office building with retail
space at street level. The scale gradually
steps down in height, complementing the
size and orientation of adjacent buildings,
and creates a strong identity through its
massing, materials, and detailing.
Thirty-seven townhouses, with a
landscaped interior courtyard behind,
continue the layering and like uses from
public to private spaces: front doors face
front doors, back doors face back doors,
and backyards face backyards.

Whitney/Grove has a small 72-car parking
garage for residents, as well as a five-level,
625-car facility located nearby on Grove
Street. The major façade of the large
parking garage is four and a half stories
tall, with a rusticated cast stone base and
an upper portion of brick. It is divided
into bays with window-like openings that
conceal the garage. At street level it has
a row of stores, maintaining the continuity
of the commercial life of the street.

1   Site model
2   Temple Street elevation
3   Temple Street townhouse
4   Site plan
5   Whitney Avenue elevation

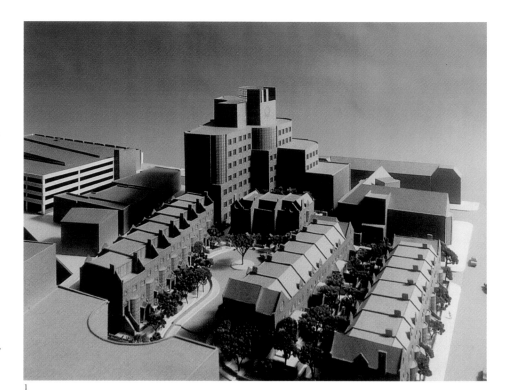

1

2

3

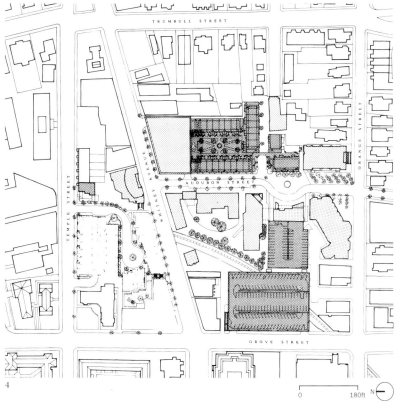

4

5

6

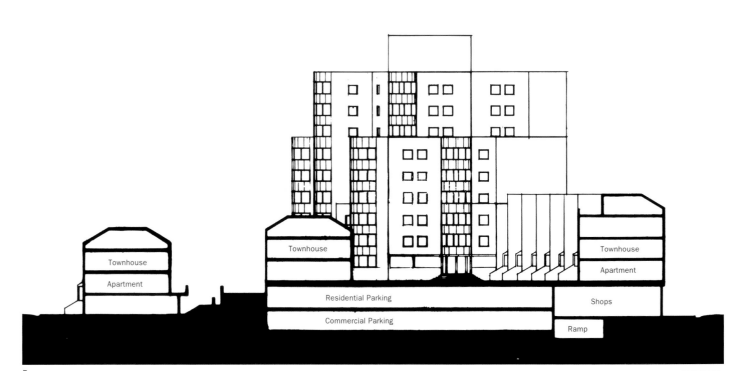

7

Townhouse		Townhouse			Townhouse
Apartment					Apartment
		Residential Parking			Shops
		Commercial Parking			
					Ramp

0   16ft

8

10

9

6   Interior courtyard
7   Section
8   Pedestrian mews
9   Townhouse interior
10 Interior courtyard

The Arts Center District
– Audubon Court

Design/Completion 1985/1988
New Haven, Connecticut
Urban Development Group/Lawrence Properties
90,000 square feet (70 luxury townhouses,
apartments, and commercial)
120,000 square feet (with parking)
Brick, precast concrete, asphalt roofing,
wood trim

Housing as a building type offers a
wonderful opportunity to help rebuild
the vernacular of a city torn by urban
decay. We have attempted to mend this
fabric through the design and master
plan of Audubon Court.

Audubon Court encloses a group of
townhouse condominiums and apartments
above ground floor commercial space.
The court has a central green—one of
the two interior courtyards in the Arts
Center District master plan that replicates
Yale University's nearby quadrangles—
providing both community and security
for urban living.

All townhouse front doors face the
green, a quiet open space that serves as
an "outdoor living room," while street
level store fronts accommodate retail
shops open to the public. Through its
gabled brick facades, it continues the
vernacular urban residential character
of the existing neighborhood.

A 70-car garage located at grade provides
parking for residents, while an adjacent
five-story parking garage serves the whole
Arts Center area.

1

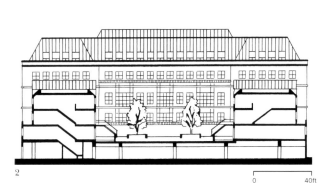

2

3

0   40ft

1   Audubon Street rendering
2   Section
3   Audubon Street
4   Pedestrian access to courtyard
5   Site plan
6   Courtyard

4

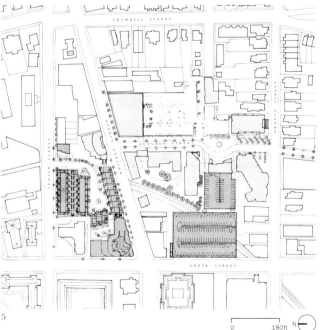

5

6

0   180ft   N

Broadway District

Design/Completion 1992/1996
New Haven, Connecticut
Yale University
8 acres
Brick sidewalks; asphalt roads; ornamental cast iron fences and street/pedestrian lights; granite curbs, decorative edges, and benches; painted steel and glass bus shelter; American elm trees

Our design attempts to restore meaningful aspects from the past to bring back the Broadway District's sense of place, yet equip its infrastructure for the future. When the replanted American elms mature, Broadway will become a truly great place.

Broadway District was a flourishing retail precinct during the late nineteenth and early twentieth centuries, but the area's pedestrian vitality was eroded by parking lots and traffic problems. The City of New Haven and Yale University jointly developed a project to revive the district, asking us to do the design.

The parking island is now sequestered within a ring of American elm trees, the wonder of Broadway in the nineteenth century, and enclosed in new painted steel fencing, a replica of the fencing that encircles the New Haven Green. We redesigned the roads to improve traffic flow, provided a number of safe pedestrian crossings, more clearly defined the sidewalks, and increased curbside parking spaces adjacent to the stores.

To give the streetscape pedestrian scale, we buried the utility lines, widened and paved the sidewalks, narrowed the road pavement, installed new kiosks, bus shelters, street furniture and lighting, and planted elm trees. We enlarged the existing Soldier's Monument Park and created a new "market island" to encourage street market activity. We hope a new shed, which we also designed, will one day be built here.

Re-established as a significant place within the fabric of New Haven, the Broadway District thrives at the confluence of urban and campus life.

1 Site plan
2 Crosswalk looking north
3 Soldier's Monument Park Circa 1907
4 Broadway Circa 1905
5 Site model
6 Market island seating
7 Expanded Soldier's Monument Park

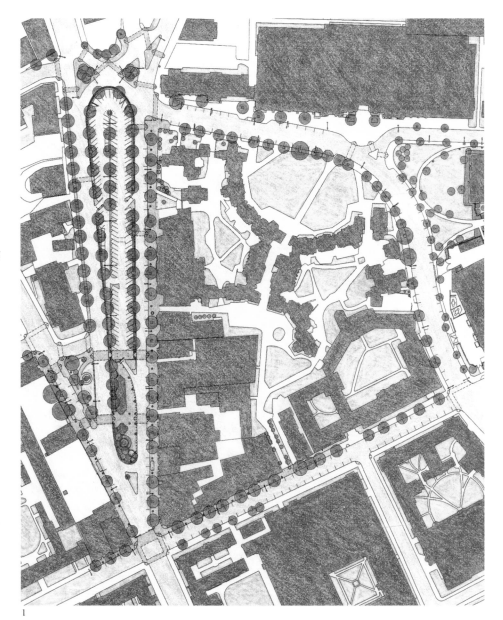

1

2

3

4

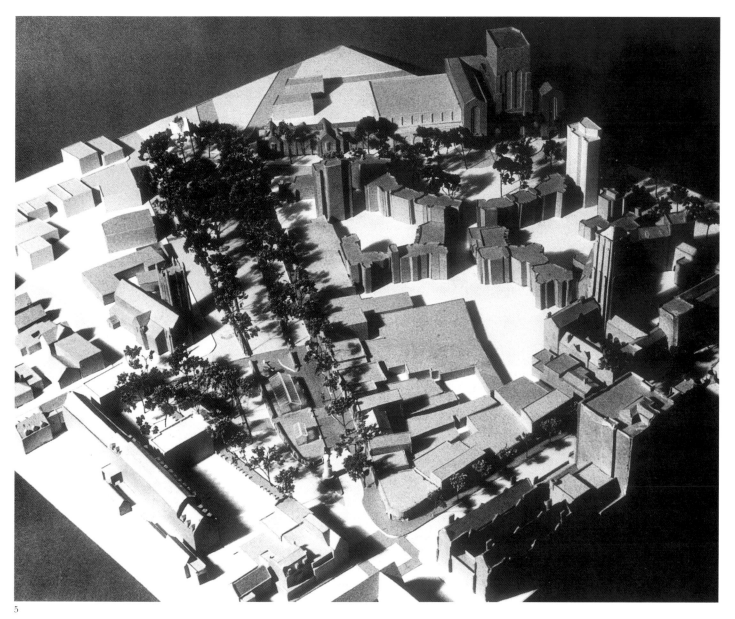

5

6

7

Southfield Village

Design/Completion 1997/2001
Stamford, Connecticut
Beacon/Corcoran Jennison Partners
166,000 square feet/330 apartments
Wood frame construction

The large existing street trees in this project are wonderful. Our street plan preserves almost all of them to retain the real "architecture" of the neighborhood.

The Southfield Village revitalization project attempts to solve the problem of creating a neighborhood to replace a "housing project." It transforms a deteriorating public housing site into a mixed-income neighborhood that integrates subsidized and market-rate housing into the larger community. Our intent is to create a neighborhood with a center.

The design incorporates into the program low-density housing units of varying architectural character, the extension of neighborhood street patterns, and clearly defined public and private spaces. All buildings will range in height from two to four stories. Family units are at grade, either flats or two-story townhouses. One-bedroom flats are above grade and are accessible by elevator. Single-family houses will be clustered at the edge of the village to form a transition in density from the neighboring streets to the central development area. All units have curbside parking for residents.

The creation of a clearly defined public realm (streets) and a private realm (rear and front yards) help to make a seamless transition into the larger neighborhood. As a measure of security and community-building, park and recreation spaces are faced by houses and interior courtyards are gated.

1 Computer rendering
2 Aerial of site
3 Site plan

1

2

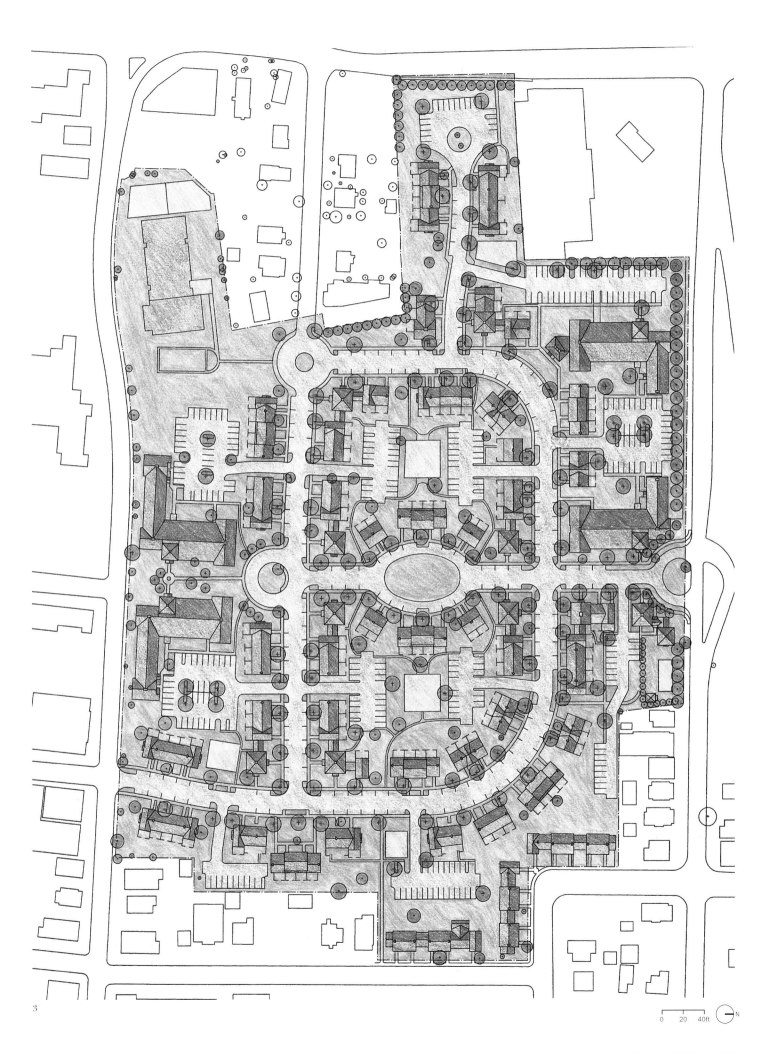

Ninth Square District

Design/Completion 1989/1995
New Haven, Connecticut
The Ninth Square Project Limited Partnership
21,500 square feet
Precast concrete, brick, aluminum store fronts
Synthetic stucco, quarry tile, carpet
and vinyl floors

The streets are the most important spaces in cities. In the Ninth Square we made new retail spaces on the ground floor and housing above to inject new life into the streets. The housing is now fully occupied, but the retail is just starting to work as downtown New Haven reinvents itself as a 24-hour restaurant and entertainment district.

New Haven was one of the first New World settlements to begin with a town plan— a grid of nine blocks, or squares, with the town green at its center. The Ninth Square has a rich past and a quality of architecture that has deemed it a National Historic District. By the late 1980s, however, it had succumbed to urban blight. A plan for renewal was developed that identified housing as the key to restoring life to the district.

In collaboration with Smith Edwards Architects, we rehabilitated virtually all of the historic four- to six-story buildings within the three-block district, and sited new buildings on vacant lots between them, integrating retail and residential ground floor spaces with apartments above. More than half of the apartments were reserved for low- to moderate-income tenants, and one large courtyard was turned into a residential community center.

Sited at an irregular intersection of two main streets, the highest new apartment building has a 12-story tower and protruding wings, making it a prominent landmark. We restored the streets with new paving, curbs, sidewalks and lighting, and built two new parking garages in the mercantile style of the district. The sidewalks are lined with plaques, designed by Sheila deBretteville. These commemorate people who have lived and worked in the Ninth Square throughout its 350-year history.

1

Before

2

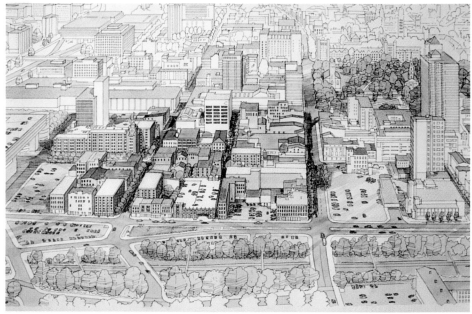
3

1 State Street Garage facade
2 State Street Garage
3 Site rendering
4 View of tower from Orange Street
5 Project site plan
6 Urban features plan

4

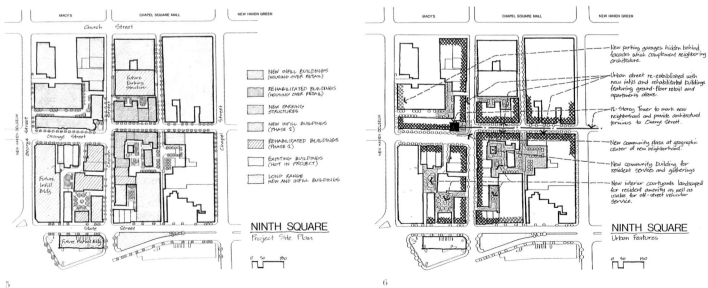

MACY'S   CHAPEL SQUARE MALL   NEW HAVEN GREEN

Church   Street

Future
Parking
Structure

Orange   Street

Future
Infill
Bldg.

State   Street

Future Market Bldg.

☐ NEW INFILL BUILDINGS
(HOUSING OVER RETAIL)

▦ REHABILITATED BUILDINGS
(HOUSING OVER RETAIL)

▨ NEW PARKING
STRUCTURES

☐ NEW INFILL BUILDINGS
(PHASE 2)

▧ REHABILITATED BUILDINGS
(PHASE 2)

☐ EXISTING BUILDINGS
(NOT IN PROJECT)

☐ LONG RANGE
NEW AND INFILL BUILDINGS

NINTH SQUARE
Project Site Plan

0 50 150

5

MACY'S   CHAPEL SQUARE MALL   NEW HAVEN GREEN

New parking garages hidden behind
facades which complement neighboring
architecture.

Urban street re-established with
new infill and rehabilitated buildings
featuring ground-floor retail and
apartments above.

12-Storey Tower to mark new
neighborhood and provide architectural
terminus to Orange Street.

New community plaza at geographic
center of new neighborhood.

New community building for
resident services and gatherings.

New interior courtyards landscaped
for resident amenity as well as
usable for off-street vehicular
service.

NINTH SQUARE
Urban Features

0 50 150

6

Firm Profile

Herbert S Newman and Partners, P.C.

Founded in 1964, Herbert S Newman and Partners is a collaborative partnership led by Herbert S. Newman, Robert Godshall, Joseph Schiffer, Michael Raso, Richard Munday, Peter Newman, and Mavis Terry.

The firm has completed a wide variety of private and public projects throughout the United States, establishing a national reputation for the design of new buildings and the renovation and restoration of existing buildings within several architectural types, including academic, corporate, institutional, religious, and urban design.

The firm is most widely known for its campus architecture; its libraries, student centers, residential and dining halls, classrooms, and athletic centers can be found at American colleges, universities, and independent and public schools across the country. This expertise in designing collegial settings has also won the firm many corporate and institutional projects.

Since its inception, Herbert S Newman and Partners has dedicated itself to a humanistic approach to architectural design, having developed an understanding and appreciation of human psychology, behavior patterns, and community-building through its work with students and clients. The idea that the primacy of space, clarity of path and structure, luminance of natural light, and humanizing quality of natural materials are essential in making a lasting, beneficial impact on the built environment in which people live, work, and play, is a tenet of the firm's work.

Having completed a substantial body of urban design projects, Herbert S Newman and Partners has worked to reinvigorate the fabric of the urban landscape, most notably in New Haven, Connecticut. The firm has received over 60 awards for design excellence, and five national AIA awards for design excellence. The firm's work has appeared regularly in architectural journals in the United States and internationally.

Biographies

Herbert S. Newman

Herbert Newman was born in New York City in 1934. After receiving his Bachelor of Arts in American Civilization from Brown University in 1955, he attended the Yale University School of Architecture. Upon receiving his Master of Architecture from Yale in 1959, he was awarded the Eero Saarinen Traveling Fellowship for Academic Excellence.

Mr. Newman began his career as an architectural designer with I.M. Pei and Partners in New York, working on international projects including Place Ville Marie. He established his own practice in New Haven in 1964, collaborating for a ten-year period with Edward Larrabee Barnes as Planning Consultant to Yale University. He has also taught continuously at the Yale School of Architecture since 1964.

Throughout his years in New Haven, Herbert Newman's contributions to the fabric of the city have included the restored and expanded City Hall, and the award-winning restorations of Union Station, Yale University Law School Library, Battell Chapel, and the Yale Center for American Arts. A catalyst for urban renewal with the development of such projects as Chapel Square Mall, Science Park, Ninth Square, Downtown South/Hill North, the Arts Center District, the Dixwell Community Center, and the revitalized Broadway District, Mr. Newman has helped define a new level of Yale–New Haven partnerships. He is actively engaged in educational, civic, and philanthropic works.

Honored in 1981 for his contributions to the profession by being named a Fellow of the American Institute of Architects, he has also served as State Commissioner of Design for the Connecticut Society of Architecture. In 1995, Mr. Newman received the Thomas Jefferson Award for Public Architecture, a lifetime achievement award bestowed by the American Institute of Architects, honoring his career and contributions to the planning and design of public spaces.

His work has received over 60 awards for design excellence, including five National American Institute of Architects Awards for Design Excellence, and has been published internationally in *Global Architecture, Architektur & Wohen, Casa Vogue, The New York Times Magazine, Architectural Record, Progressive Architecture, Architecture Magazine*, and others.

Mr. Newman has authored articles for numerous publications, including the *Journal of Architectural Education, American School & University*, and *Architecture Magazine*, and has served as visiting critic, juror, and lecturer at Carnegie-Mellon University, Harvard University, Columbia University, and the University of Tennessee. In 1999 his firm presented the symposium "Architecture in Residence: Enhancing the Quality of Residential Life."

Robert Godshall

Robert Godshall received his undergraduate education at Dartmouth College, and his architectural education at Yale University. He joined Herbert S Newman and Partners in 1974 as a designer and became a Partner in 1990.

Mr. Godshall has collaborated with Mr. Newman in the planning and design of many of the firm's award-winning academic and institutional projects, including Colgate University Library and Residence Halls; Dartmouth College Residential Cluster; Yale University Sterling Law Library and Lecture Hall; the Old Campus renovations at Yale University; the new Residence Hall at Yale University; University of Connecticut Northwest Quadrangle Dining Hall and Dormitories; renovation and expansion to the Maritime Aquarium at Norwalk; and the Ninth Square Residential Development in New Haven.

Mr. Godshall has served as a critic at the Yale School of Architecture, the University of Nebraska School of Architecture, and Dartmouth College. His lectures have covered topics ranging from community and campus planning and design to design-build project delivery. He was an organizer and co-presenter of Herbert S Newman and Partners' 1999 symposium on emerging ideas in student residential planning and design on American college campuses: "Architecture in Residence: Enhancing the Quality of Residential Life."

Joseph Schiffer

Joseph Schiffer received his Bachelor of Architecture degree from the Cooper Union School of Architecture in 1967. He joined Herbert S Newman and Partners in 1974 and became a Partner in 1990.

Mr. Schiffer has been a principal in the planning and design of many of the firm's award-winning projects including Duracell World Headquarters; The Pocantico Conference Center of the Rockefeller Brothers Fund; Yale University Art Gallery, Center for American Art; the Performing Arts Center at Greenwich Academy; Yale University School of Organization and Management, Donaldson Commons; and Wesleyan University's Freeman Athletic Center. He has collaborated closely with Herbert Newman on projects including the Scandling Student Center at Hobart & William Smith Colleges; Alfred University's College of Business and Administration; the New School for Social Research; and the Guilford Community Center.

His teaching experience includes an assistant professorship in Architectural Design at Paier College of Art, and visiting juror status at Columbia University and Cooper Union School of Architecture. His lectures and published works cover topics ranging from planning community and student centers to implementing sustainable design and construction techniques in new buildings. He is an organizer and co-presenter of Herbert S Newman and Partners' 1999 residential life symposium: "Architecture in Residence: Enhancing the Quality of Residential Life."

Michael Raso

Michael Raso studied architecture and engineering at the University of New Haven and Roger Williams College. He joined Herbert S Newman and Partners in 1975, became an Associate in 1985, a Senior Associate in 1990, and a Partner in 1994.

Mr. Raso has focused on much of the firm's restoration and renovation work at Yale University including the Old Campus, Bingham Hall, Sterling Law School renovations, and the Central Power Plant expansion. He has worked closely with Herbert Newman on the firm's award-winning projects including the Lynn University Library and ASSAF Academic Building; the Residence Village at Eastern Connecticut State University; and the Jewish Religious Center at Williams College. His work on urban projects includes the Ninth Square Subsidized Housing Renovation; Whitney/Grove Square Mixed-Use Development in New Haven; Eastfield Mall Renovation in Eastfield; Dania Jai Alai; SeaFair Restaurant and Retail Development; and residences including Snyder, Crocker and Round Hill.

Richard Munday

Richard Munday graduated with a Bachelor of Architecture degree from Adelaide University in Australia in 1978 and a Master of Environmental Design from Yale University in 1985. Prior to coming to the U.S. in 1983, he taught in the architecture school at the Royal Melbourne Institute of Technology, was co-editor and publisher of the Australian architecture journal *Transition*, and was in private architectural practice. In 1981 he was a recipient of the President's Award to Young Architects from the Royal Australian Institute of Architects, Victoria Chapter.

Mr. Munday joined Herbert S Newman and Partners in 1985 as Senior Designer, became an Associate in 1990, Senior Associate in 1998, and a Partner in 1999. He works closely with Herbert Newman in the master planning and design of new and renovated public school, institutional, and academic projects. His work with the firm includes renovations and additions to the New Haven City Hall, Lynn University Library, the New School for Social Research, Yale Medical School offices, the Maritime Aquarium at Norwalk, numerous public schools, and master planning projects including Downtown South Mixed-use Development in New Haven, Connecticut, and the Mizner Park Study.

Mr. Munday has served as visiting critic at the Rhode Island School of Design, and design critic at the Royal Melbourne Institute of Technology.

Mavis B. Terry

A graduate of Quinnipiac College in Hamden, Connecticut, and a business consultant, Mavis Terry joined the firm as Business Manager in 1980, becoming a Partner in 1994.

Directing all non-technical aspects of the firm's business, Ms. Terry's role is to facilitate and manage the firm's operations, including financial management, human resource administration, non-technical staff supervision, and the administration of retirement plans.

Peter Newman

Peter Newman received his Bachelor of Fine Arts degree from Boston College in 1983. Prior to architectural school, Mr. Newman had his own set design practice, specializing in television commercials and industrial films. He received a Master of Architecture degree at Yale University in 1990, and a certificate in Architectural History from the University of Florence, Italy. He served as Project Architect at Yale University until 1993. He joined Herbert S Newman and Partners in 1993, becoming an Associate in 1997.

His work with the firm ranges from design to master planning on projects including the new Residence Hall at Yale University, the addition and modernization of the Yale Power Plant, and the Lynn University Library and ASSAF Academic Building in Boca Raton, Florida. His work on institutional projects includes the Pocantico Conference Center of the Rockefeller Brothers Fund and The Maritime Aquarium at Norwalk. He is responsible for business development and client contact for the firm, as well as directing its marketing endeavors, including the firm's 1999 residential life symposium: "Architecture in Residence: Enhancing the Quality of Residential Life." Mr. Newman is responsible for the art direction of the firm's publications, including this monograph.

He has served as facilitator and instructor for the Architectural Resource Center, educating elementary school children in cognitive development and problem solving through design.

Don Cosham

Don Cosham graduated from Rennselaer Polytechnic Institute in 1964 with a Bachelor of Architecture degree. His early career as a designer included work with Prentice and Chan, Ohlhausen in New York City. He joined Herbert S Newman and Partners in 1974 as Project Architect, became Vice President in 1980, and a Partner in 1990.

His work with the firm includes New Haven's Union Station; New Haven City Hall; Westport Public Library; University of Rochester Eastman School of Music Student Living Center; Williams College Jewish Religious Center; Colgate University Library, Dining Hall and Dormitories; Lynn University Library; Bridgeport Federal Courthouse; Milford Jai Alai; Teletrack Theater; Dania Jai Alai; and the SeaFair Waterfront Marketplace. He has worked closely with Herbert Newman on many of the firm's Yale University projects including Battell Chapel, the Old Campus Renovations, the Golf Clubhouse, and Sterling Law School Library and Lecture Hall.

Mr. Cosham retired in 1996. He has frequently consulted with Herbert S Newman and Partners on projects including The Maritime Aquarium at Norwalk; Yale University Residence Hall; Conard High School; William H. Hall High School; West Hills/ Conte School; and the University of Connecticut Northwest Quadrangle Dining Hall and Dormitories.

Glenn H. Gregg

Glenn Gregg attended Texas A&M University from 1959 to 1962 and received his Master of Architecture degree from the Yale University School of Architecture in 1967. While at Yale, he received the Feldman Prize in 1966, and was a Paris Prize nominee in 1967.

Mr. Gregg joined Herbert S Newman and Partners in 1969, became an Associate in 1971, and a Partner in 1974. In his 12 years with the firm he worked closely with Mr. Newman on the planning and design of projects including Yale University Old Campus renovations; the Yale University Art Gallery, Center for American Art; Milford Jai Alai; Teletrack Theater; and Colgate University, Dana Addition, Case Library.

William Newhall

William Newhall received his undergraduate and professional education at Yale University. He received a Master of Architecture degree in 1970. He joined the firm in 1970, became Vice President in 1980, a Partner in 1990, and remained a principal with the firm until his death in 1992.

Among Mr. Newhall's work with the firm are award-winning projects including Yale University Art Gallery, Center for American Art; Cullman Indoor Tennis Courts; Milford Jai Alai; Northeastern University Law School, Kariotis Hall; Taft School Arts and Humanities Building and Residence Hall; and the Arts Center District in New Haven.

Partners, Associates & Staff

Partners are denoted in **bold**
Associates are denoted in *italics*

Diane Abbott
Nancy Adelson
Jonathan Alger
Sally Allison
Jay Alpert
Edward Alshut
Nicola Armster
Isabel Askenase
Elizabeth Augustyn
David Ball
Maynard Ball
Jeffrey Barber
David Barkin
George Barnes
Michael Barone
Scott Bates
Christopher Beardsley
John Paul Beck
Sally Beeman
Kevin Bennett
Ann Benton
Phillip Bernstein
John Boecker
Holly Bollier
David Bono
Kenneth Boroson
Robert Bostwick
Mari Bowman
Peter Bowman
Natalie Bradley
Evelyn Bravata
Daniel Brodhead
Samuel Brooke
Philip Brooks
Daniel Brown
Mary Buck
Michael Cadwell
Ewa Buttolph
Alice Calabrese
John Carruth
Daniel Cecil
Michael Chasse
Gordon Christopher
Janet Chuang
Louise Clark
Richard Clarke
Peter Clement
Georges Clermont
Abbey Cohen
Lauren Condon
Peter Conrad
Michael Coppola
Don Cosham
David Cote
Mark Cote
Doris Cronan
Timothy Culvahouse
Steven Currie
Charlene Curry

Michael Davis
Roberta DeAlba
Dennis DeLorenzo
Mary Jean Dempsey
Ellen Denisevich
Eugenie Devine
David Dickinson
Raymond Dickinson
Lenore DiGioia
Mary DiStefano
Karyl Dokos
Carlos Dominguez
Catherine Donnelly
Joseph Dorais
Mimi D'Orazio
Douglas Dover
Kelly Drew
May Dunn-Palensky
David Edwards
Katherine Edwards
William Egan
James Elmasry
Gwendolyn Emery
David Epstein
Trudy Erickson
Peter Ernst
Amy Estabrook-Ross
Alison Ewing
Shawn Fanning
Laura Fedro
Joseph Ferrucci
Kurt Flegler
Joanna Fowler
Kathryn Frederick
Tara Gaffney
Samuel Gardner
Donald Giannini
Ellen Gillooly
Tamar Gisis
Robert Godshall
Camilo Gonzalez
Suzanne Greenbaum
Glenn Gregg
Nathan Hadley
Mary Jane Haesche
Gary Hale
Leonard Hall
Daniel Harazim
Andrew Hardenbergh
Russell Hatfield
Angela Hatley
Howard Hebel
Patricia Hefner
Jose Hernandez
Michelle Herrick
Joan Hogan
Michael Homer
Tae Hong
John Hooker

Toyota Horiguchi
Michael Horowitz
Lance Hosey
David Hotson
Marc Houston
Joseph Huether
Dana Hunter
Mira Hyde
Barbara Ince
Joan Jaggar
Michael Jasper
Matthew Johnson
R. Wade Johnson
Kristin Jones
Maitland Jones
Stuart Joseph
Idris Kadrican
Steven Kahn
John Kaliski
Martin Kapell
Jeffrey Kaufman
Daniel Keating
Steven Keedle
Marieanne Khoury-Vogt
Jung Gon Kim
Sam Kirby
Karen Knisely
Philip Koether
Peter Kohn
Jane Kolleeny
Barbara Kretschmer
Terry Krobot
Kathy Kuryla-Holt
Maki Kuwayana
Mark Lally
Robert Lamothe
Evangeline Lampadarios
Steven Lapin
Mark Leach
Eun Lee
Hsun Hung Lee
Yoonhie Lee
Gary Levene
Kelli Levesque
Michael Levy
Deborah Lewis-Dowdy
Colin Livesay
Guy Livingston
Thomas Lodge
Robert Lord
Drew Maciag
Peter MacPartland
William Marcano
Cynthia Mario
Evan Markiewicz
Elizabeth Martin
Martin Mata
Ann McCallum
Julia McCarthy

Keith McCormack
Robert McCoy
Mary Alison McMahon
Thomas Meehan
Nestor Melnyk
Freida Menzer
Oscar Mertz
Jeffrey Miles
Marsden Moran
Kevin Morrison
Philip Mosciski
Rainer Muhlbauer
Richard Munday
Casandra Murphy
Ralph Nelson
Sara Nelson
William Newhall
Edna Newman
Herbert Newman
Peter Newman
Rashida Ng
Walter Nicolai
Sara Nomellini
Kari Nordstrom
Mark Odell
John Orfield
Randall Ott
Mark Outman
Tracy Page
Jeffrey Palmer
Ronald Paolillo
Lance Parker
Thomas Paulsen
Susan Personette
Mary Pniakowski
Yann Poisson
Jeffrey Potash
Efendi Rashkuyev
Michael Raso
Richard Raso
James Reilly
Nancy Restivo
Rebecca Reynolds
Mimi Ricci
Lynn Robbins
Charles Roberts
Roberta Robson
David Rodrigues
Marisol Roman
Suzanne Roos
David Rosenbloom
Peggy Rubens-Duhl
Joseph Rufrano
Frank Ryan
Heberton Ryan
Roger Schickedantz
Joseph Schiffer
Peter Schubin
Peter Schuerch

Ian Scott
Donna Scymanski
Jae Shim
Lisa Side
Rupinder Singh
Janyce Siress
Bretherton Sleeper
Brian Smith
Kevin Smith
Warren Smith
David Snyder
Jill Sparks
Steven Starr
Linda Stimson
Scott Stober
Pierre Strauch
Gilbert Strickler
Willie Ma Sung
Michael Susarchick
Lindsay Suter
P. Barry Svigals
Charles Swanson
Michael Syrotinski
Sahoko Tamagawa
Washington Taylor
Mavis Terry
Raymond Terry
Jennifer Tobias
Nathan Topf
Julie Trachtenberg
Paul Treadwell
Mimi Tsai
Dade Van Der Werf
Jan Van Loan
Agatha Vastakis
William Vinyard
John Virostek
Curtis Wagner
David Walker
Sally Wallian
Jill Ward
Eric Watson
Stephen Weeks
Carl Welty
Carl Wies
Richard Wies
Marjorie Wilkinson
Dawn Williams
Gail Wilshire
Robert Wilson
Matthew Wittmer
Jocelyn Wolfe
Mai Wu
Stephen Zane
David Zenner
Hong Zheng
Olga Zureczko

Collaborators & Consultants

Associated Architects

Bennett Sullivan Associates and Uri Shetrit: B'nai Israel Synagogue

Charles E. Moore & Associates: Tower East, New Haven

Cooper Carry, Inc.: Mizner Park

Edward Cherry: Dixwell Community Housing

Edward Larrabee Barnes/John M.Y. Lee & Partners, Architects: Yale University Campus Planning and Old Campus Renovations

Ehrenkrantz & Eckstut Architects: Stamford Redevelopment Master Plan

Jay Alpert Architects: Greater New Haven Jewish Community Center

Ricci Associates: New Haven Correctional Center

Skidmore, Owings & Merrill: New Haven Union Station

Smith Edwards Architects: Ninth Square District

Consultants

A. Grant Thornbrough & Assoc. (landscape architects)

Ace Design (exhibit designers)

Acentech, Inc. (acoustic consultants)

ACF, Inc.

Acorn Consulting Engineers (mechanical, electrical, plumbing consultants)

Adler Consulting, Inc. (traffic consultants)

Ahern Builders (general contractor)

Alford Associates, Inc. (civil engineers)

Allan Davis Associates (civil engineers/ traffic consultants)

Altieri Sebor Wieber (mechanical, electrical, plumbing consultants)

Andrew Hidi & Associates (mechanical engineers)

ATC Environmental, Inc. (asbestos consultants)

Babinsky & Klein (mechanical, electrical, plumbing consultants)

Barakos-Landino, Inc. (civil engineers/ traffic consultants)

Barnhart, Johnson, Francis & Wild, Inc. (structural engineers)

BBN Lab (acoustic consultants)

Bill Gillenwater (estimator)

Birchfield Foodsystems, Inc. (food consultants)

Boston Concessions Group (food consultants)

BPD Roof Consulting, Inc. (roof consultants)

Brabham Debay and MacDonald (mechanical electrical engineers)

Bruce J. Spiewak, Architect (code consultant)

Bruce Whitney Sielaff, AIA (laboratory consultants)

Burge Consultants (interior designers)

Business Food Services (food consultants)

BVH Engineers (mechanical, electrical, plumbing consultants)

C & R Engineering (electrical engineering consultants)

Caci System Designs, Inc. (security consultants)

Cama Incorporated (furniture consultants)

Cecil & Rizvi (civil engineers)

The Center for Engineering (civil engineers)

Chapman Ducibella Associates (security consultants)

Charles Cosler Theatre Design (theater consultants)

Charles R. Wilson Engineers (mechanical, electrical, plumbing consultants)

Chartwell Company (estimators)

Cini-Little International, Inc. (food consultants)

Clarence Blair Associates (civil engineers)

Codespoti Associates (surveyors)

Communications Cable Consultants Incorporated (telecommunications consultants)

Construction Specification, Inc. (specification writers)

Consul-Tech Engineers (civil engineers)

Consulting Engineering Services (mechanical electrical engineers)

Con-Test (asbestos consultants)

Cosentini Associates (mechanical, electrical, plumbing consultants)

Crabtree-McGrath Associates (food consultants)

Daedalus Projects, Inc. (estimators)

David Rosenbloom/Synthesis Design Visualization (renderer)

DeCarlo & Doll, Inc. (civil engineers)

Deirdre Schiffer (graphic designer)

DiBlasi Aschettino, P.C. (structural engineers)

Diversified Technologies Consultants (mechanical, electrical, plumbing consultants/civil engineers)

Dober Lidsky Craig and Associates, Inc. (programming consultants)

Donald Baerman, AIA, Architect (specification writers)

Donald Bliss (lighting consultant)

Donald Jensen & Associates (structural engineers)

Dr. Clarence Welti, P.C. (geotechnical consultants)

E.A. Rae & Associates, Ltd. (electrical engineering consultants)

Edward Wheeler, CCS, CSI (specification writers)

Eisenberg Associates (code consultants)

Electronic System Associates (electronic systems consultants)

F.A. Hesketh & Associates, Inc. (surveyors)

F.M. Costantino, Inc. (renderers)

Falcone Fine Art Studio (renderers)

Fitzpatrick Design Group, Inc. (interiors consultant)

Flack + Kurtz (mechanical/electrical engineers)

Fraser & Fassler (mechanical, electrical, plumbing consultants)

Gelbart Company (renderers)

General Drafting & Design (mechanical, electrical, plumbing consultants)

Gibble Norden Champion Consult Eng., Inc. (structural engineers)

Girard & Co. - Engineers (structural engineers)

H.B. Fishman & Co., Inc. (roof consultants)

Haines Lundberg Waehler, Architects (interior consultants)

Haley & Aldrich, Inc. (geotechnical consultants)

Hanscomb, Inc. (estimators)

Harry Van Deusen (landscape architects)

Harwood Wallace Loomis (code consultants)

Helenski-Zimmerer Associates (mechanical, electrical, plumbing consultants)

Hendriks Associates, LLC (civil engineers)

Hofbauer Associates, Inc. (mechanical engineers)

Hubert Hayes (elevator consultant)

Huntington Company (civil engineers)

I. Shiffman Consulting Engineers (mechanical, electrical, plumbing consultants)

I.K. Chann Associates (traffic consultants)

Integrated Security Systems (security consultants)
Jack Curtis (landscape architects)
James McFarland and Associates, Inc. (food consultants)
Jenkins & Charland, Inc. (structural engineers)
Jenkins & Huntington, Inc. (elevator consultants)
Jerry Kugler (lighting consultant)
John A. Van Deusen & Associates, Inc. (elevator consultants)
John C. Martin Consulting Engineer (structural engineers)
John Christen (mechanical, electrical, plumbing consultants)
John Stopen (structural engineers)
Joseph R. Loring & Associates (mechanical, electrical, plumbing consultants)
Julia Gelbart (interior designer)
K.A. LeClair (surveyors)
Kallen & Lemelson (mechanical, electrical, plumbing consultants)
Kazmar Associates (structural engineers)
Klepper, Hahn & Hyatt (structural/civil engineers)
Kuljian Corporation (mechanical electrical engineers)
Langan Engineering (civil engineers)
LaSalle Partners Development Ltd. (development consultant)
Leavitt Associates, Inc. (envelope/forensics consultant)
Lemessurier/Sci (electrical engineering consultants)
Leslie Buckingham (estimators)
Lev Zetlin Associates (civil engineers)
Lockwood Greene Engineers, Inc. (engineers)
Luchini-Milfort Goodell & Assoc. (mechanical, electrical, plumbing consultants)
LZA Group (mechanical, electrical, plumbing consultants)
Mallory-Stair (interior design consultants)
McCall & Lynch, Architects and Planners (architects)
McColl Wade (mechancial engineers)
McDonald and Debay (mechanical electrical engineers)
McDonald/Sharpe & Associates, Inc. (civil engineers)
McPhail/Lemessu (mechancial engineers)

Melchiori Associates (mechanical, electrical, plumbing consultants)
Mesh/Juul (lighting consultant)
Michael Horton & Associates (structural engineers)
Michelin Construction Services, Inc. (estimators)
Novicki (electrical engineering consultants)
Nutting Engineers of Florida (geotechnical consultants)
Oppenheim/Lewis (estimators)
ORCA (exhibition engineers)
Otis Elevator (elevator consultants)
Parsons Brinckerhoff (mechanical, electrical, plumbing consultants/structural engineers)
Peter Szilagyi (mechanical, electrical, plumbing consultants)
Playcon Enterprises (athletic consultants)
Polytech (mechanical, electrical, plumbing consultants)
Professional Construction Services, Inc. (estimators)
Purcell Associates (civil engineers)
R. G. Vanderweil Engineers, Inc. (mechanical electrical engineers)
Ray Firmin Cost Consultants (estimators)
Raymond/Raymond Associates (food consultants)
Redniss and Mead (civil engineers)
Rhodes/Dahl (cost estimators)
Ricci Associates (architects)
Richard J. Adams (surveyors)
Robert Hurwit & Associates, Inc. (model makers)
Robson & Woese, Inc. (mechanical, electrical, plumbing consultants)
Rocco V. D'Andrea, Inc. (civil engineers)
Rolf Jensen & Associates, Inc. (fire consultants)
Rolland/Towers, P.C. (landscape architects)
Ron Eichorn Design (lighting consultants)
RPM Systems, Inc. (lighting consultant)
Rumney Associates (graphic designers)
Rykoff-Sexton (food consultants)
Santo Domingo Consulting Engineers (structural engineers)
Sasaki Associates (civil engineers)
Schiff & Associates (security consultants)
Sealy Stephenson Value & Knecht (engineering consultants)
Selbert Design Associates (landscape architects)

Shen, Milsom & Wilke, Inc. (acoustic consultants)
Sheremeta Associates, Inc. (civil engineers)
Sigmund Kei (mechanical, electrical, plumbing consultants)
Simpson Gumpertz & Heger, Inc. (envelope/forensics/structural consultants)
Sippican Consultants Inc. (structural engineers)
Special Testing Laboratory, Inc. (testing consultants)
Spiegel, Zamecnik & Shah, Inc. (structural engineers)
Strong Cohen (graphic designers)
SWA Group (landscape architects)
Sylvan R. Schemitz & Associates, Inc. (lighting consultants)
Syska & Hennessy (mechanical/electrical engineers)
TAMS Consultants, Inc. (mechanical, electrical, plumbing consultants)
Technical Design Assoc. (mechanical engineers)
Theatre Projects Consultants, Inc. (theater consultants)
Thomas D. Ricca Associates (food consultants)
Tor Smolen Calini and Anastos (structural engineers)
Torrenti Engineers, PC (structural engineers)
TPA Design Group (landscape architects)
Tremaine Lighting (lighting consultant)
Turner Construction Company (construction managers)
United Architects, Architects (interior consultants)
URS Greiner (civil engineers/surveyors)
VanZelm, Heywood & Shadford (mechanical, electrical, plumbing consultants)
Walker Parking Consultants (parking and traffic consultants)
Wesco Fountains (landscape architects)
William H. Rowe and Associates (mechanical/electrical engineers)
Wolf and Company (estimators)
Yale University Engineering Services (mechanical, electrical, plumbing consultants)
Zion & Breen (landscape architects)

General Contractors & Construction Managers

ALCA Construction Company (general contractor)

Bartlett Brainard Eacott (construction managers)

Brennan Construction Company (construction managers)

C. F. Wooding (construction managers)

C.J. Fucci Construction (general contractor)

CDS, Inc. (construction managers)

Chase Enterprises (construction managers)

The Dimeo Companies (construction managers)

E&F Construction Co. (construction managers)

Fontaine Brothers (general contractor)

Frank L. Ciminelli (construction managers)

Fusco Corporation (construction managers)

Gerrits Construction (general contractor)

Gilbane Building Company (construction managers)

Giordano Construction Co., Inc. (construction managers)

Hueber-Breuer Construction Co. (construction managers)

J. D. Taylor (general contractor)

Jackson Construction (general contractor)

James J. Welch (construction managers)

John M. Lightfoot, Inc. (general contractor)

Joseph Kelly (general contractor)

Larson Construction Management Company (construction managers)

Leach Building Company (construction managers)

Lehrer McGovern Bovis, Inc. (construction managers)

McGuire & Bennett (construction managers)

McGuire Group (construction managers)

Morganti, Inc. (general contractor)

O&G Industries, Inc. (construction managers)

P. Francini Co. (general contractor)

Panza Construction (general contractor)

Pavarini Construction Co., Inc. (construction managers)

Peter Prizio, Inc. (general contractor)

Pike Company (general contractor)

Schnip Development Corporation (general contractor)

Stone Building Company (general contractor)

Tishman Construction Corporation (construction managers)

Tomlinson Hawley Patterson, Inc. (construction managers)

TRITEC Real Estate Company, Inc. (construction managers)

W.E. O'Neil Construction Company (general contractor)

Walsh Construction Company (construction managers)

Chronological List of Buildings & Projects

* indicates work featured in this book

HERBERT S NEWMAN AND PARTNERS

1962–1969

Winnick Residence*	1962
Budget Liquors	1964
Woodbridge Country Club	1966
Gant Shirt Factory*	1967
Dr. and Mrs. Herbert Kaufman Residence	1967
Dixwell Community House	1968
Forest Hills Pro Shop	1969

Woodbridge Country Club

Dixwell Community House

1970–1972

Edith B. Johnson Towers	1970
Lytton Residence	1970
Schackne Residence	1970
Turtle Motors	1971
Winnick, Resnick, Skolnick and Auerbach Law Office	1972
Yale University, Cullman Indoor Tennis Courts*	1972

Lytton Residence

Lytton Residence

1973

Brown Brothers Showroom	1973
Hotchkiss School Tennis Center	1973
West Rock Tennis Center	1973
Yale University Co-op	1973
Yale University, Golf Cart Shelter	1973
Yale University, Pierson/Sage Parking	1973

Yale University Co-op

Yale University, Golf Clubhouse

1974–1975

Heritage Village Conference Center	1974
Milford Jai Alai*	1974
Quinnipiac River Housing	1974
Yale University Art Gallery, Center for American Arts*	1974
Galt Toys	1975
Norfolk Music Shed/Painting Studio	1975
William T. Rowe Towers	1975
Yale U., Old Campus Lawrance Hall*	1975
Yale U., Old Campus Welch Hall*	1975

Galt Toys

William T. Rowe Towers

1976–1977

Milford Orthopedic Surgical Assn.	1976	Kantor Addition	1977	
Teletrack Theater*	1976	Naiman Residence Art Gallery	1977	
Yale University, Sterling Law School		Naiman Physical Therapy Suite	1977	
Library and Lecture Hall*	1976	Tower East	1977	
Yale U., Old Campus McClellan Hall*	1976	Yale U., Old Campus, Farnham Hall,		
Beth El Synagogue, Troy, New York	1977	Durfee Hall, Vanderbilt Hall*	1977	
Guilford Tennis & Swim Club		Yale University, School of		
Pool House	1977	Organisation and Management,		
		Donaldson Commons*	1977	

Beth El Synagogue

1978

Beth El Synagogue, Fairfield, CT	1978
Buteau Dentist Office	1978
Dania Jai Alai	1978
Greene Street Condominium	
Conversion	1978
Taft School	
Cruikshank Athletic Center	1978

Buteau Dentist Office

Dania Jai Alai

1979

Clifford Beers Clinic	1979	U.S. Department of the Navy,	
Colgate University, Dana Addition,		Groton, Submarine Base Handball	
Case Library*	1979	Courts	1979
Connecticut Junior Republic	1979		
Fabriyaz Showrooms	1979		
Family Affair Restaurant,			
Greenburgh	1979		

Connecticut Junior Republic

1980–1981

Blumberg, Whitten & Sherry	
Office Building	1980
Halcyon Office Building	1980
Haviland Parking Deck	1980
New Haven Union Station*	1980
Northeastern University Law School,	
Kariotis Hall*	1980
Yale University, Coxe Cage	
Field House*	1980
Yale University, Soccer/Lacrosse	
Stadium*	1980
Boca Raton Housing	1981
Colgate University, Curtis Frank	
Dining Hall*	1981
Cohen & Wolf Law Offices	1981
Family Affair Restaurant, Yonkers	1981
First Federal Bank, Cheshire	1981
First Federal Bank, Fairfield	1981
Kramer Residence*	1981
Polivy Residence	1981
Snyder Residence	1981

First Federal Bank, Cheshire

Snyder Residence, Florida

Cohen & Wolf Law Offices

1982–1983

SeaFair Waterfront Marketplace

Hough Office Building

Il Villano Restaurant

Hopkins Athletic Facility

1984–1985

Shorr Residence

State Street Office Building

Golf View Master Plan

Brenner, Salzman, Wallman & Goldman Law Offices

Middlebury College, Student Center

Downtown South Master Plan

1986–1987

Bic Drive Office Building   1986
Kent School, South Point Dormitory   1986
Mizner Park Master Plan   1986
University of Rochester,
Eastman School of Music,
Student Living Center*   1986
Yale University, Bowl Press Box*   1986
IBM Corporation, Middlebury
Feasibility Study   1987
Middlesex Community College   1987
Taft School, Residence Hall*   1987
Wesleyan University, Boat House   1987
Science Park Master Plan   1987
Wesleyan University,
Freeman Athletic Center*   1987

Middlesex Commmunity College

Kent School, South Point Dormitory

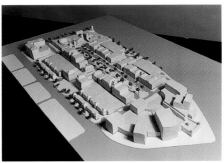
Mizner Park Master Plan

Yale University, Bowl Press Box

1988

Arts Center District – Whitney/Grove* 1988
AT&T Office Building   1988
Bridgeport Federal Courthouse
Annex*   1988
Bridgeport Superior Courthouse   1988
Crocker Residence   1988
D'Andrea Building   1988
Ebersol Residence   1988
Elm Haven Housing Master Plan   1988
Greater New Haven Jewish
Community Center   1988
Williams College, Dormitory Study   1988
Williams College Jewish Religious
Center*   1988
Yale University, Calhoun College*   1988

Bridgeport Superior Court

AT&T Office Building

Crocker Residence

Ebersol Residence

1989–1993

Yale University Medical School, Administrative Offices

Cornell University, Noyes Center Dining Hall

Elliptipar Showroom

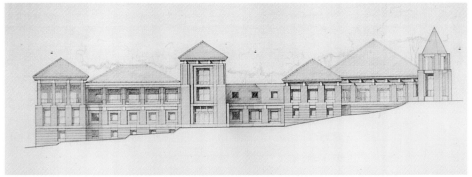

Alfred University Campus Center (study)

U.S. Postal Service, Wallingford

Yale University, Silliman College/Byers Hall (before)

Yale University, Silliman College/Byers Hall (after)

1994– 1997

Loomis Chaffee School, Athletic Facilities Master Plan

Loomis Chaffee School, Squash Courts

Choate Rosemary Hall, Archbold Hall (before)

Choate Rosemary Hall, Archbold Hall (after)

Eastern Connecticut State University, Residential Village

Eastern Connecticut State University, Residential Village

New Haven Jewish Community Center

New Haven Jewish Community Center interior

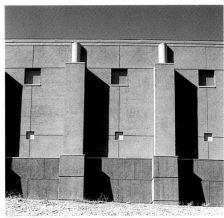
New Haven Jewish Community Center detail

1998–1999

Amherst College, Kirby Theater

Mercantile Exchange at Chelsea Harbor Hotel

New Haven Gateway Proposal (Church St Bridge before)

New Haven Gateway Proposal (Church St Bridge after)

New Haven Gateway Proposal (Chapel Sq. Mall before)

New Haven Gateway Proposal (Chapel Sq. Mall after)

Selected Awards, Competitions & Exhibitions

Awards

Record House Award for Design Excellence
Architectural Record
Winnick Residence
1965

Design Citation
Progressive Architecture
Gant Shirt Factory
1969

Honor Award for Design Excellence
American Institute of Architects/
Connecticut
Dixwell Community Center
1972

Record Interiors Award for Design Excellence
Architectural Record
Yale University, Cullman Indoor Tennis Courts
1974

National Honor Award for Design Excellence
American Institute of Architects
Yale University Art Gallery, Center for American Arts
1979

Excellence in Architecture Award
American Institute of Architects/
Connecticut
Yale University, Sterling Law School Library
1979

Excellence in Architecture Award
American Institute of Architects/
Connecticut
Milford Jai Alai
1979

National Honor Award for Design Excellence
American Institute of Steel Construction
Milford Jai Alai
1979

Excellence in Architecture Award
American Institute of Architects/
Connecticut
Teletrack Theater
1980

Excellence in Architecture Award
American Institute of Architects/
Connecticut
Yale University, School of Organization and Management,
Donaldson Commons
1980

National Honor Award for Design Excellence
American Institute of Architects/
American Library Association
Yale University, Sterling Law School Library
1980

Award for Athletic Facilities Design
American Institute of Architects/
Connecticut
Yale University, Coxe Cage Field House
1981

Regional Interiors Award
American Institute of Architects/
Connecticut
Teletrack Theater
1981

First Honor Award
American Wood Council
Connecticut Junior Republic
1981

Excellence in Architecture Award
American Institute of Architects/
Connecticut
Colgate Library, Dana Addition, Case Library
1982

Merit Award
New Haven Preservation Trust
Clifford Beers Clinic
1982

National Honor Award for Design Excellence
American Institute of Architects/
American Library Association
Colgate University, Dana Addition, Case Library
1983

Architectural Citation
National School Boards Association
Colgate University, Dana Addition, Case Library
1983

Small Building Award
American Concrete Institute, New England Chapter
Northeastern University Law School, Kariotis Hall
1984

Architectural Citation
New England Real Estate Directory
Cohen & Wolf Law Offices
1984

Architectural Citation
American School & University Architectural Portfolio
Northeastern University Law School, Kariotis Hall
1984

Honor Award for Design Excellence
American Institute of Architects/
Connecticut
Yale University, Battell Chapel
1985

Record House Award for Design Excellence
Architectural Record
Round Hill Residence
1985

Builder's Choice Grand Award
Builder Magazine
The Crossing at Blind Brook
1985

Builder's Choice Honorable Mention
Builder Magazine
Round Hill Residence
1985

Renaissance Honorable Mention Award
Remodeling Magazine
Cohen & Wolf Law Offices
1985

Renaissance Special Commendation Award
Remodeling Magazine
Yale University, Battell Chapel
1985

Renaissance Grand Award
Remodeling Magazine
Chapel Square Mall
1985

National Honor Award for Design Excellence
American Institute of Architects
Yale University, Battell Chapel
1986

Unbuilt Projects Award
American Institute of Architects/
Connecticut
New Haven City Hall
1986

Renaissance Best of the Year Award
Remodeling Magazine
Boca Raton Residence, Florida
1987

Renaissance Merit Award for Design Excellence
Remodeling Magazine
Taft School, Arts and Humanities Building
1987

Design Award
American Institute of Architects/
Connecticut
SeaFair Waterfront Marketplace
1988

Design Award
American Institute of Architects/
Connecticut
Taft School, Arts and Humanities Building
1988

Honor Award for Design Excellence
American Institute of Architects/
Connecticut
Brenner, Saltzman, Wallman & Goldman
Law Office
1989

Public Space Honor Award
American Institute of Architects/
Connecticut
New Haven Union Station
1989

Excellence Awards Program
Masonry Institute of Connecticut
Arts Center District—Whitney/Grove
1989

Builder's Choice Merit Award
Builder Magazine
Arts Center District—Whitney/Grove
1989

International Honor Award for Design Excellence
Interfaith Forum of Religion, Art, and
Architecture/
American Institute of Architects
Williams College Jewish Religious Center
1991

The David B. Perini Award for Project Team Effectiveness
Kent School Dormitory
1991

Design Award
American Institute of Architects/New
England Regional Council
New Haven Union Station
1991

Builder's Choice Grand Award
Builder Magazine
Taft School, Residence Hall
1991

Facility of Merit Award
Athletic Business Magazine
Wesleyan University, Freeman Athletic
Center
1991

National Historic Preservation Award
President George Bush's Advisory Council
on Historic Preservation
New Haven Union Station
1992

Honor Award for Design Excellence
American Institute of Architects/
Connecticut
Williams College Jewish Religious Center
1992

Unbuilt Projects Honor Award
American Institute of Architects/
Connecticut
New School for Social Research
1992

Design Award
American Institute of Architects/New
England Regional Council
Williams College Jewish Religious Center
1993

Honor Award for Design Excellence
Society of American Registered Architects
Hobart and William Smith Colleges,
Scandling Student Center
1993

Outstanding Achievement Award
Associated Builders and Contractors
Kent School Dormitory
1993

Honor Award for Design Excellence
American Institute of Architects/
Connecticut
The Pocantico Conference Center of the
Rockefeller Brothers Fund
1994

The Thomas Jefferson Award for Public Architecture
American Institute of Architects
Lifetime Achievement Award
1995

National Honor Award for Urban Design
American Institute of Architects
Ninth Square District
1995

Honor Award for Design Excellence
American Institute of Architects/
Connecticut
Ninth Square District
1995

**National Honor Award for Design
Excellence**
American Concrete Institute
Colgate University, Drake Hall
1995

Preservation Award
Connecticut Trust for Historic
Preservation
Ninth Square District
1995

Building Award
American Concrete Institute, New
England Chapter
Ninth Square District
1995

Honor Award for Design Excellence
American Institute of Architects/
Connecticut
New Haven City Hall
1996

Design Award for Best Mixed-Use Facility
Precast/Prestressed Concrete Institute
Ninth Square District
1996

Sustainable Design Award
Boston Society of Architects
Duracell World Headquarters
1997

Certificate of Recognition
Connecticut Building Congress
Duracell World Headquarters
1997

Certificate of Recognition
Connecticut Building Congress
Ninth Square District
1997

Post-Secondary Citation
*American School & University Architectural
Portfolio*
Lynn University Library
1997

Design Award Citation
American Institute of Architects/
Connecticut
Duracell World Headquarters
1998

AIA Top Ten Environmental Solutions
American Institute of Architects
Duracell World Headquarters
1999

Honor Award for Design Excellence
American Institute of Architects/
Connecticut
Lynn University Library and ASSAF
Classroom Building
1999

Honor Award for Design Excellence
American Institute of Architects/
Connecticut
Broadway District, New Haven
1999

Competitions

Winning Entry
Edith B. Johnson Towers
1969

Winning Entry
William T. Rowe, Elderly Housing
1971

Winning Entry
Teletrack Theater
1976

Winning Entry
Northeastern University Law School,
Kariotis Hall
1979

Winning Entry
Western Connecticut State University,
Residential Village
1994

Winning Entry
Eastern Connecticut State University,
Residential Village
1996

Winning Entry
Yale University, New Residence Hall
1997

Exhibitions

Yale University Faculty Show
Yale University School of Architecture
New Haven, Connecticut
September 1991

New-New England Architecture
Boston Society of Architects
Boston, Massachusetts
June 1992

Technical College Exhibition
Middlesex Community Technical College
Middletown, Connecticut
November 1995

New England Architects
Boston Society of Architects
Boston, Massachusetts
November 1997

**1998 American Architecture Awards
Exhibit**
The Chicago Athenaeum: Museum of
Architecture and Design
Chicago, Illinois
Summer 1998

Yale University Faculty Show
Yale University School of Architecture
New Haven, Connecticut
November 1998

New England Architects
Boston Society of Architects
Boston, Massachusetts
November 1998

New England Architects
Boston Society of Architects
Boston, Massachusetts
November 1999

Selected Bibliography

"AIA Honor Awards Urban Design." *Architecture* (May 1996). (Ninth Square District)

Altman, Mary Ann. "Renovating Historic Buildings." *The National Law Journal Office Design for Law Firms* (April 1985). (Cohen & Wolf Law Offices)

Architects of the Millennium. Melbourne, Australia: The Images Publishing Group, 2000. (Yale University, New Residence Hall; Richard's of Greenwich; Greenwich Academy, Wallace Performing Arts Center/New Athletic Center; Conard High School)

Architects of the United States of America. Vol. 2. Melbourne, Australia: The Images Publishing Group, 1991.

"Award Winning Architecture." *The Connecticut Architect* (Spring 1981). (Yale University School of Management, Donaldson Commons; Teletrack Theater)

Bararan, Regina S. "Splendid Spaces." *Food Management* (April 1990). (Yale University, Calhoun College Dining Hall)

Bass, Paul. "Restored Mall Delights New Haven." *The New York Times* (December 2, 1984). (Chapel Square Mall)

"Best Mixed-Use Facility: The Ninth Square, New Haven, Connecticut." *Ascent* (Fall 1996).

Bingham, Michael C. "The Ghost of Christmas Passed: Seeking Salvation for Our Cities: Why Architect Herbert Newman Thinks Urban Centers Like New Haven Haven't Outlived Their Usefulness." *Business New Haven* (January 2, 1996).

Bradford, Susan & June Fletcher. "Builder's Choice." *Builder* (October 1991). (Taft School Arts & Humanities Building)

Charles, Eleanor. "A $9-Million Expansion for Norwalk's Aquarium." *The New York Times, 1999 Real Estate, In the Region/ Connecticut* (May 2, 1999), p. 9. (Maritime Aquarium at Norwalk)

Charles, Eleanor. "Running Mom and Pop off Glitzy Greenwich Avenue." *The New York Times, Sunday* (September 14, 1997). (Richard's of Greenwich)

Charles, Eleanor. "Yale in the Midst of a Mammoth Renovation Program." *The New York Times, Sunday* (October 12, 1997). (Yale University Master Planning, Residential Colleges, New Residence Hall)

Charles, Eleanor. "Yale Works to Break Down the Town–Gown Barrier." *The New York Times, Connecticut Section* (September 25, 1994). (Broadway District)

Colurso, Mary. "Master Builder: Skyscraper Architect Thinks Small." *New Haven Register* (January 21, 1993). (Herbert S. Newman profiled as recipient of Habitat for Humanity Master Builder Award)

"Common Ground." *Architectural Record* (October 1989). (Dartmouth College, East Wheelock Residential Cluster)

"Company Profile: Herbert S. Newman and Partners, AIA, P.C." *Connecticut Architect & Specifier* (January 1989). (Downtown South/Hill North; Yale University, Battell Chapel; Wesleyan University, Freeman Athletic Center; Colgate University, Dana Addition, Case Library; New School for Social Research; University of Rochester, Eastman School of Music, Student Living Center; Dartmouth College, East Wheelock Residential Cluster; Arts Center – Audubon Court)

"Connecticut Junior Republic School, Dining Hall and Offices, Litchfield, Connecticut." *Architectural Record* (June 1981).

Consiglio, Laura. "New Haven: A Refurbished Union Station Gives the City the Gateway it Deserves." *Yale Alumni Magazine* (February 1987).

Crosbie, Michael J. "A Brotherhood of Geometric Parts." *Architecture* (June 1986). (Colgate University, Curtis Frank Dining Hall)

Crosbie, Michael J. "For the Greater Good." *The Hartford Courant* (July 17, 1994). (New Haven City Hall)

Crosbie, Michael J. "Green Architecture Epitomized: Bethel's Duracell Building Makes Excellent Use of Surroundings." *Hartford Courant* (April 1996). (Duracell World Headquarters)

Crosbie, Michael J. "Quiet Places Sewn into the City: Two Residential Complexes in New Haven, Herbert S. Newman, FAIA." *Architecture* (1989). (Whitney/Grove & Audubon Court)

Crosbie, Michael J. "Richness of Decoration Restored." *Architecture* (June 1986). (Yale University, Battell Chapel)

Daniels, Lee A. "Country Town Houses in Westchester." *The New York Times* (November 4, 1983). (Crossing at Blind Brook)

Deitz, Paula. "Where Rockefeller Found Culture." *Financial Times Weekend* (May 14–15, 1994). (Pocantico Conference Center of the Rockefeller Brothers Fund)

Demkin, Joseph A., AIA *Environmental Resource Guide.* New York: John Wiley & Sons, Washington, D.C.: American Institute of Architects, 1997. (Duracell World Headquarters)

Dunnington, Ann. "Like a Phoenix: New Haven Inaugurates a Comprehensive Revitalization Scheme Firmly Based in Preservation." *Historic Preservation News* (December 1994 – January 1995). (Ninth Square District)

Edwards, Livingston A. "Herbert S. Newman." *Live Magazine* (1985). (Cohen & Wolf Law Offices; Round Hill Residence; Colgate University; SeaFair Waterfront Marketplace; and Hobart & William Smith College, Scandling Student Center)

First House. Whitney Library of Design, New Jersey: Princeton Architectural Press, 2000.

"Five Honored by AIA." *Progressive Architecture* (February 1995). (Herbert S. Newman receives Thomas Jefferson Award)

Freeman, Allen. "The Coming of Kykuit." *Historic Preservation* (July–August 1992). (Pocantico Conference Center of the Rockefeller Brothers Fund)

"Freeman Athletic Center: The Place to Be," "Putting It All Together," and "Light, Space, Confluence." *Wesleyan Alumni Magazine* (Winter 1991). (Wesleyan University, Freeman Athletic Center)

"From Coaches to Conference." *Architectural Record* (February 1995). (Pocantico Conference Center of the Rockefeller Brothers Fund)

Gamrecki, John. "Hobart & William Smith Colleges: The Scandling Center." *Food Management* (January 1985).

Garbarine, Rachelle. "A New Neighborhood Is Rising in New Haven." *The New York Times* (n.d.) (Ninth Square District)

Hart, Sara. "Guess Who's Going Green?" *Architecture* (August 1998). (Duracell World Headquarters)

"Grand Award: The Crossing at Blind Brook." *Builder* (October 1985).

"Honor Award: New Construction." *Interfaith Forum on Religion, Art & Architecture* (Winter 1991–92). (Williams College Jewish Religious Center)

"Housing for the Yalies." *Up front, Interiors* (November 1997). (Yale University, New Residence Hall)

International Architecture Yearbook. Vol. 1. Melbourne, Australia: The Images Publishing Group, 1995. (Bridgeport Federal Courthouse; Pocantico Conference Center of the Rockefeller Brothers Fund)

International Architecture Yearbook. Vol. 3. Melbourne, Australia: The Images Publishing Group, 1997. (Duracell World Headquarters)

International Architecture Yearbook. Vol. 4. Melbourne, Australia: The Images Publishing Group, 1997. (Colgate University, Drake & Curtis Halls; Lynn University Library)

International Architecture Yearbook. Vol. 5. Melbourne, Australia: The Images Publishing Group, 1999. (New Haven City Hall)

Kipphut, Janet. "New-look Mall an Extension of Green." *New Haven Register* (October 28, 1984). (Chapel Square Mall)

Kirby, John B. "Old Yale: The Chapel is Restored to Splendor." *Yale Alumni Magazine* (December 1984). (Yale University, Battell Chapel)

"Libraries: Beyond Bookshelves." *College Planning & Management* (February 1999). (Lynn University Library)

"Lynn University Library." *Library Journal Architectural* (December 1997).

"Lynn University, Boca Raton, Florida." *American School & University Architectural Portfolio 1997* (November 1997).

Mason, Katrina R. & Ann Marie Moriarty. "Renaissance '87." *Remodeling* (January 1988). (Snyder Residence)

McCall, Pete. "AIA Honors Tri-State Projects." *New York Construction News* (March 4, 1996). (Ninth Square District)

McGrath, Norman. *Photographing Buildings Inside and Out.* 1st Edn. Whitney Library of Design, 1987. (Round Hill Residence)

McGrath, Norman. *Photographing Buildings Inside and Out.* 2nd Edn. Whitney Library of Design, 1993. (Round Hill Residence)

"Milford Jai Alai: Festive Building for 'Merry Festival'." *Architectural Record* (April 1978).

Miller, Robert L. "The New Haven City Hall: A Revived Symbol and an Urban Catalyst." *Connecticut Architect & Specifier* (January 1989). (New Haven City Hall)

"A New Auditorium and Exhibition Space for the Art Gallery at Yale University." *Architectural Record* (May 1978).

"A New Frontispiece Transforms a College Library." *Architectural Record* (September 1982). (Colgate University, Dana Addition, Case Library)

"New Haven Complex Demonstrates Precast Concrete's Superiority in Multi-Unit Residential Buildings." *PCI Journal* (January–February 1995). (Ninth Square District)

"New Residence Hall to be Built at Yale University." *Architectural Record* (December 1997).

"P/A Inquiry: Remaking Malls." *Progressive Architecture* (November 1988). (Chapel Square Mall)

"A Phoenix of a Library." *Yale Alumni Magazine* (May 1994). (Yale University, Silliman College)

"Pinwheel Plan Provides Privacy." *House Beautiful's Building Manual* (Fall–Winter 1965–66). (Winnick Residence)

"A Pivotal Placemaker." *Architectural Record* (November 1983). (Northeastern University Law School, Kariotis Hall)

"Private Enterprise Embraces Sustainable Design." *Architectural Record* (October 1997). (Duracell World Headquarters)

"Record Houses 1956–1966: A Decade of Significant Innovation." *Architectural Record* (February 1966). (Winnick Residence)

"Record Houses of 1965." *Architectural Record* (1965). (Winnick Residence)

"Record Interiors of 1974." *Architectural Record* (January 1974). (Yale University, Cullman Indoor Tennis Courts)

"Remodel of Split Level House into Mediterranean Villa a Stunning Transformation." *Sun/Coast Architect/ Builder* (May 1988). (Snyder Residence)

"Residence Village." *IMI Today* (November–December 1997). (Eastern Connecticut State University, Residential Village)

Residential Spaces of the World: A Pictorial Review of Residential Interiors. Vol. 1. Melbourne, Australia: The Images Publishing Group, 1994. (Round Hill Residence; Crocker Residence; Kramer Residence)

"Restoring a Chapel's Original Splendor." *Remodeling* (July 1986). (Yale University, Battell Chapel)

"Return to Splendor." *American School & University* (September 1979). (Yale University Law School, Library & Lecture Hall)

"Round Hill, Woodbridge, Connecticut by Herbert S. Newman." *Architectural Record Houses of 1985.*

Scully, Vincent. *American Architecture and Urbanism.* New York: Henry Holt and Company, 1988. (New Haven City Hall)

"SeaFair Creates Exciting Gateway to Water's Edge." *Sun/Coast Architect/ Builder* (June 1988).

Sedlacek, Frantisek (ed.). *Award Winning Architecture International Yearbook 1997.* Munich: Prestel-Verlag, 1997. (Ninth Square District)

"Shopping Mall Rehabilitation." *Progressive Architecture* (November 1988). (Chapel Square Mall)

Shutt, Craig A. "Precast Cuts Time, Costs on Multi-Housing Project." *Ascent* (Winter 1996). (Ninth Square District)

Sommerhoff, Emilie Worthen. "Raise High the Recycled Roof Beams, Carpenters." *Facilities Design & Management* (November 1998). (Duracell World Headquarters)

"'Swing Dorm' Taking Shape." *Yale Alumni Magazine* (October 1997). (Yale University, New Residence Hall)

"Tower of Light." *Connecticut Magazine* (August 1986). (Round Hill Residence)

Trainor, Gene. "New Haven Project to Improve Broadway Area." *Connecticut Post* (September 12, 1993). (Broadway District)

"Two Differing and Remarkable New Projects by Herbert Newman Associates for the Old Interiors of Yale." *Architectural Record* (July 1979). (Yale University Law School, Library & Lecture Hall)

"Two Pluses for the Town: Richards Move to Add Parking …" *Greenwich Magazine* (September 1997). (Richards of Greenwich)

"Urban Community Centers." *Progressive Architecture* (April 1972). (Dixwell Community Center)

"View-Capturing Angles for a Clearing in the Woods." *Building Manual* (Fall–Winter 1976–77). (Lytton Residence)

Watts, Katherine. "Architect Profile: Herbert S. Newman and Partners, P.C." *New England Construction News* (July 7, 1994).

Weiss, Stephen. "The New New Haven." *New England's Real Estate Magazine* (March/April 1989). (Downtown South)

"The Winner's Circle in New Haven." *Architectural Record* (February 1981). (Teletrack Theater)

World Residential Design. Vol. 1. Japan: N.I.C Ltd., 1990. (Round Hill Residence)

"Yale Translates an Abandoned Chapel as a New Commons." *Architectural Record* (January 1981). (Yale University School of Organization & Management, Donaldson Commons)

"Yale University is Preserving its Great Late 19th-Century Architecture by Remodeling the Old Campus." *Architectural Record* (March 1977).

Zonderman, Jon. "The Remaking of Calhoun." *Yale Alumni Magazine* (May 1989). (Yale University, Calhoun College)

Acknowledgments

To my wife, Edna, who recognized before me that I should be an architect and who, by ultimatum, decreed it.

To my children and their families, my thanks for sharing precious time with architecture.

To my students and faculty colleagues, from whom I have taken more than given.

To my partners and collaborators, my thanks for patience, perseverance, and the giving of the best in each of you to make our work together exciting, and to make work better than any of us could do alone.

Regarding this monograph, a special thanks to Peter Newman for his eye and skill in composing these pages; to Richard Munday for his thoughtful editing and writing; to Lisa Side for her skillful management of the process; to Julie Trachtenberg for her work in organizing the visual material; to Lindsay Suter and Rupinder Singh for their expertise in revitalizing many old drawings. Pat Shoemaker, a gifted graphic designer, gave order to our collection of images.

Special appreciation to Paul Latham and Alessina Brooks of The Images Publishing Group, their staff and Rod Gilbert of The Graphic Image Studio.

Photography Credits:

Peter Aaron/Esto: 38 (1,2); 39 (4); 40 (5); 41 (7–9); 42 (1,2); 43 (5); 44 (6–8); 45 (9); 66 (2); 67 (3); 68 (8–10); 69 (11–13)

Robert Benson: 18 (2); 19 (3); 20–21; 22 (6); 23 (8); 24 (9); 25 (10–12); 72 (2); 73 (3,5); 90–91 (1); 94 (7,8,10); 95 (11,12); 98 (1–3); 103 (3); 108 (1,2); 142 (2); 143 (3,4); 144 (5); 145 (7); 146–147; 148 (2); 150 (1–3); 152 (2); 153 (3); 163 (2,3); 164 (5); 165 (7,9); 225 (4); 226 (2); 227 (6,7)

Ron Blunt: 120 (18); 121 (22)

Dan Cornish/Esto: 26 (3); 27 (4)

Ambrose Cucinotto: 184 (1,2); 185 (3)

Thomas Delbeck: 10 (1–3); 11 (4); 12 (6); 13 (7); 14-15; 16 (1); 17 (2)

Scott Francis/Esto: 46 (2,3); 47; 48 (6,7); 49 (8,9)

Fred George: 126 (1); 127 (3); 128 (4); 129 (7); 130 (9,10); 131 (11)

Jeff Goldberg/Esto: 92 (2); 93 (4,5); 94 (9); 95 (13,14); 122 (2,3); 123 (4); 124 (7–9); 125

Michael Marsland: 87

Norman McGrath: 18 (1); 50 (1,2); 51; 52–53; 54 (7,8); 55; 82 (1,2); 83 (3); 84 (2); 85; 96 (3,4); 97 (5); 112 (2,3); 113; 114 (6); 115 (7); 116 (8,9); 117 (10–12); 118 (13,15); 119 (16); 120 (19–21); 138 (2); 139 (3–5); 154 (1); 155 (3); 172 (1,2); 174 (2,3); 175 (5-7); 176–177; 179 (3,4); 180 (6); 181 (8); 194 (2); 195 (4); 196–197; 208 (1,2); 209 (3); 211; 212–213; 214 (9-10);215; 216 (13); 217; 230 (1,2); 231 (4)

Joseph W. Molitor: 202 (1); 203 (4)

David Ottenstein: 158 (2); 159 (3); 160 (5); 161

Robert Perron: 80 (1); 81

Steve Rosenthal: 132 (2); 133 (3); 134–135: 136 (5–7); 137 (10); 188 (2,3); 189; 190 (5); 191 (8–10); 192–193; 220 (2); 221 (3,5); 222 (6); 223 (8–10); 224 (3): 225 (6)

Nick Wheeler: 28 (1,2); 29 (3); 30 (6); 31 (7,8); 32 (1,2); 33 (3); 34–35; 36 (6); 37 (7,9); 56 (1); 57 (2); 58–59; 60 (6-8); 61 (10); 62 (3); 63 (4); 64 (6-8); 65 (9); 76 (2); 77 (3,6); 78 (7); 79 (11); 168–169; 170 (2,3); 171 (4,6); 204 (1); 205; 206 (7,8); 207 (9)

Rendering Credits:

Maynard Ball: 129 (8)

Frank Costantino: 151 (4)

Abraham Gelbart: 100 (1); 164 (6); 199 (4); 230 (3)

David Rosenbloom: 71 (3); 141 (3)

Staff photograph by Mimi Houston: 232

All other images by permission Herbert S Newman and Partners

Index

Bold page numbers refer to projects included in
Selected and Current Works